LEAD THE WAY

Authentic Leadership for the Next Generation

Philip Mion

Lead The Way: Authentic Leadership for the Next Generation
Published by Legacy Press

ISBN (Paperback): 979-8-9943540-0-1
ISBN (eBook): 979-8-9943540-1-8

Printed in the United States of America
First Edition 2026

Praise for Lead the Way

Phil Mion, in my opinion, is one of the best youth leaders around. He has devoted many years of his life to raising up the leaders of tomorrow. This book is the fruit of those years. It is eminently practical, easily readable, thoroughly Biblical, and powerfully inspirational. And it is totally grounded in the local church. It should be required reading for anyone called to youth ministry in these challenging days.

David Campbell, Pastor, Author, and Professor at Theos University.

Phil is a true and beautiful gift to the Kingdom of God. With a unique understanding of emerging culture and a mature Kingdom wisdom, he is well equipped to help the next generation into Biblical and fruitful leadership rhythms. I'm excited about the way God will use this resource in your and your team's life.

Dan Lian, Associate Pastor at Newspring Church

Phil Mion is my favorite Youth Pastor in America. For over a decade, he's given his life to building the local Church, reaching students, and empowering the next generation of leaders. As a leader you want to learn from a leader who has been there and gets it. Phil is that leader, and this is the book you need.

Jonathan Rivera, Campus Pastor at Southeastern University

There are far too few books from dynamic young leaders carrying a serious local-church vision. In an age of church skepticism, this book is a prophetic intervention. Phil has written a work that should be required reading for every church staff member on earth.

Nathan Finochio, Founder of Theos University

Lead the Way is the kind of book leaders reach for when they feel the weight of forming the next generation and want something more than hype. Philip Mion writes with Scripture in one hand and real life in the other, offering a steady, practical path through character, community, and culture that rings true for parents, pastors, and anyone who serves young people. If you want leadership that tells the truth, stays humble, and actually helps, this is a strong guide.

Chris Palmer, PhD Dean, Professor Barnett College of Ministry & Theology Southeastern University

I have watched Phil Mion lead young people with faithfulness, authenticity, and genuine love for nearly a decade. He has exceeded every expectation and in turn our youth ministry has become a place of revival. Lead the Way captures the principles that I have seen him live that has helped him reach and shape a generation. This book is practical and a must read for anyone wanting to connect and influence the emerging generation.

Alex Sagot, Lead Pastor of Calvary Church

For my children,

Eden Luna and Jude Luis

Author's Note

The stories shared throughout this book are based on real lives, conversations, and moments of growth, struggle, and faith. To honor personal privacy and protect the individuals involved, names and identifying details have been changed. In some cases, stories have been combined or adapted, while remaining true to the heart and essence of the experiences being shared.

These stories are not meant to elevate individuals but to highlight the greater work that God is doing in and through the next generation. I hope that readers will see reflections of their own journeys in these pages and be encouraged to lead with conviction, humility, and faithfulness in their own contexts.

Table of Contents

Part 3 — Culture

Conclusion

FORWARD

When your child is born, you hold them in your arms and wonder who they will become. You imagine them playing sports, scraped knees, school projects, and even a few gray hairs they will give you along the way—but you never expect that one day you will be writing the foreword to their book on Christian leadership and parenting. Yet here I am, both proud and slightly stunned, trying to find words that match the weight of what my son has created.

As a father, you spend years hoping your example will speak louder than your mistakes. You pray that the seeds you plant—faith, integrity, compassion, discipline—take root somewhere deep. You hope that one day your child will grow into someone who not only knows God but *walks* with Him. Watching my son grow into a man who is now a father himself, teaching others how to lead and parent with Christ at the center, is one of the greatest honors of my life.

I am sure it is no surprise to anyone when I say this, but I did not always get parenting right. There were days I felt like I was doing more repenting than parenting. Days when patience ran thin, the pressure of this life ran high, and the only thing "Christ-like" was the prayer I whispered under my breath, asking the Lord to help—quickly. But God is gracious, and children are forgiving, and somewhere between the chaos and the lessons, something beautiful happened: we grew together.

This book reflects the growth I have had the privilege of seeing firsthand and being part of. It is thoughtful, practical, and grounded in Scripture—but it also carries my son's heart. A heart that loves God, values family, values people, and wants to see parents rise as leaders who build homes where grace is practiced, truth is taught, and love rules. In all honesty, this book is a resource I wish I had when I was raising my son and daughter.

As his father, I have watched him wrestle with his faith, mature in it, and ultimately choose to lead with humility rather than perfection. That is what makes this book special. He is not writing from a pedestal; he is writing from experience, from what he has gotten wrong and what he has gotten right. He is writing this book from the messy, funny, challenging, holy work of learning to lead a family God's way.

As you open these pages, I pray that you read not just with your mind, but with your heart. Laugh when it gets real, reflect when it gets deep, and allow God to speak to you through a son who has become a wise and faithful man.

To my son: I am proud of you, not just for writing a book, but for living one.

And to every reader: You're in good hands. Enjoy the journey. A grateful father who needs God's grace every day!

Luis Mion

Introduction

This book is about a hand-off. And the enemy wants it dropped.

Every generation is supposed to pass the torch of faith to the next. It is how legacy works. It is how the Church grows. But right now, that exchange—the hand-off from parent to child, from pastor to student, from leader to follower—is under spiritual fire.

We are seeing one of the most significant generational shifts in modern history. And the Church cannot afford to fumble it. Sure, there have been glimmers of hope and the tides have been turning, but there is still much work to be done.

The enemy is not just after the family. He is after the future. And if we do not act now with clarity, courage, and compassion, we will lose the very ones we were called to reach.

I want to challenge you to have a long-term thinking mindset. To not view this task of leading the way for the next generation as a project that will take a few months or even years, but to understand the lasting impact we have on our children, students, and ministers for 100 years from now.

Ray and Jani Ortlund authored a book titled *To the Tenth Generation* that really challenged my thinking about how I approach helping the next generation, especially as a pastor and father.

In their book, they discuss how a particular scripture prompted them to ask God to open their minds to the importance of thinking in generations. They write, "Years ago, Jani was reading her bible…when something leaped off the page. "No one is born of forbidden union may enter the assembly of the Lord. Even to the tenth generation, none of his descendants may enter the assembly of the Lord. Even to the tenth generation, none of them may enter the assembly of the Lord forever." (Deut 23:2-3), Whoa, what a thought…God excluding a group of people from entering his presence, for ten generations?"[1]

Then a new thought came to mind: "If God excluded certain people to the tenth generation, how much more does he long to include people to the tenth generation!"

We need to understand the generational blessing of God and understand that there is too much at stake for us to sit idly by as generations knowing Jesus or never knowing Jesus are at risk, and we have something to do about it!

If you do not believe the hand-off is under attack, read these real-life stories of young people who are and have been through the fire.

STORIES FROM THE FIRE

The stories you are about to read are not polished sermons or filtered Instagram reels; they are genuine accounts from real people with real lives. These are students and young adults from my local church here in Miami. They are sparks of fire—flickers of God's grace in the lives of young men and women who are wrestling with faith, doubt, and destiny in real time.

For many young people, faith does not simply vanish in a dramatic moment; instead, it often weakens and fades until God breathes life into the embers once more.

The testimonies of these young people reveal that, when their faith seemed almost extinguished, God revived it. These are their voices.

Ashley was only sixteen when her faith began to wane. Life felt like a downward spiral, and she decided to attend church one last time. Standing on the lawn, she confessed to a friend that she was done. That night during worship, she whispered to God, "I don't want to believe anymore." Then came the quietest nudge: "One more time." One more day, one more week, one more month. Step by step, God revived her faith until she found herself walking in a fresh faith, which she had not thought possible.

James never planned to take God seriously either. He was distant, drifting, and did not care much about his relationship with Jesus — until a friend invited him to a youth group. That simple invitation was the spark that changed everything. He felt God's love, found a community that became like family to him, and even wrote his college essay about how his life had been transformed.

Derek did not think God wanted anything to do with him. Depression pressed down heavily, and the voices of others told him who he was supposed to be. He believed the lie that God had abandoned him. But one night, he walked into a youth group, and something unexpected happened. He did not find a sermon that answered all his questions — he saw a group of friends who reflected God's love in how they embraced him. What felt like the end of his faith became a beginning he never saw coming. Before long, Derek was standing before his entire school, telling them how Jesus had changed his life, even if it cost him friendships.

Jenny fought a quieter battle. As a freshman, she was caught between people-pleasing and following Jesus. She tried to fit in without compromising her faith, but the tension wore her down. One night, alone in her room, she repented and turned on worship music. In that private moment, God's presence rushed in like never before. No lights, no stage, no crowd — just her and Jesus. That night, she realized she no longer needed anyone else's approval; she already had His.

Eric knew what it felt like to stand alone. One day at school, a group of students began to pray together. His friends mocked them, urging him to join in the laughter. Instead, Eric walked across the divide and stood with the ones who were praying. The cost was immediate: he lost friends. But in that moment of loneliness, he found something deeper — brothers in Christ, a spiritual family that would outlast any fragile high school friendship.

Grace nearly gave up as a leader. She loved Jesus, but every time she left church, she walked back into circles of friends who did not. It felt like she had to choose between obedience to God and belonging anywhere at all. For months, she had struggled with compromise, wondering if it was even worth trying to continue. Then came a moment at a youth and young adult Conference. Looking down her row, she saw a complete line of friends who loved Jesus, worshiping together. Tears streamed down her face as she realized: God had surrounded her with a new community. What she thought was impossible — friends who pursued Jesus wholeheartedly — had become her reality. What she almost lost to loneliness, God redeemed with family.

These stories echo like sparks in the night. Depression did not win. Compromise did not win. Loneliness did not win. When faith felt fragile, God proved faithful. He placed courage in a teenager, presence in a bedroom, and family in the middle of isolation. These are not distant testimonies — they are the voices of a generation still in the fire, choosing Jesus when everything else pulls them away.

Different stories, same truth: God does not let the fire go out. He whispers, He invites, He surrounds. Faith that seems dead can burn again.

Faith almost died, but God breathed on the embers. Students stood when it cost them. Revival spread from one voice to many. And the Spirit interrupted plans with something eternal. These are not just their stories — they are previews of what God wants to do again. The fire is spreading. The only question is: will we fan the flame, or let it die out?

WHAT THIS BOOK IS AND IS NOT

This book is not about gimmicks or trends. It is not here to bash culture or chase after relevance. It is a rally cry to the Church: If we want to reach the next generation, we must become the kind of people they want to follow.

We must be faithful when culture tells us to be flexible.

We must love without compromising the truth.

We must be grounded when everything around us is shifting.

The principles in this book are valuable for anyone working with young people, from Youth Pastors and Coaches to Teachers and parents. Regardless of your role, if you follow Jesus Christ, you are called to ministry. I appreciate believers active in schools, counseling, and athletics—your presence matters. Together, we can encourage young people to boldly live out their faith and inspire others to follow Jesus.

Now there is no shortage of content written about Gen Z and Alpha. Barna studies, Pew reports, and endless think pieces try to diagnose what is happening in teenagers' minds today. However, despite the available data, something is often missing: a voice from inside the trenches.

This is not a think tank report. It is not a lecture. This book was born from prayer, tears, and hundreds of conversations with students, youth leaders, and parents as they looked to pass on their faith to the next generation.

What follows is not a perfect formula. It is a framework. A call to live faithfully, lead wisely, and build ministries and homes that make Jesus unavoidable.

To begin, we must face reality. An ugly truth is still the truth, and the data you will see may discourage you, but that is not its purpose. Once we truly know the work that must be done and what is at stake, only then can a passion for the next generation be ignited.

THE URGENCY OF NOW

Let us look at the facts. If we want to take this issue seriously, we need to recognize how serious it is. According to the Barna Group, only 4% of Gen Z have a biblical worldview. Many teenagers say they feel lonely, anxious, and overwhelmed—even though they are more digitally connected than ever. One in three Gen Z students now identify as "nones," meaning they have no religious affiliation.[2]

We are seeing a decline in trust toward spiritual authority, while exposure to alternative ideologies is rising rapidly. It is not only external influences that affect them. Sometimes, the Church adds to the problem with moral failures, celebrity culture, and superficial teachings. Students are paying attention, and when our actions do not match our words, they notice.

We are losing them—not because they have rejected Jesus, but because we have not consistently represented Him well.

I have dedicated a large part of my life to youth ministry, starting as a student, moving into a leadership role, and serving as a youth pastor for over 16 years. One key insight I have gained is the urgent need to connect with the younger generation more than ever before. They live in a fast-changing world, marked by social media and shifting cultural norms. This environment, while full of information, often lacks real substance. The challenges faced by today's youth are unmatched. Still, it is crucial to remember that the Gospel is timeless, and Jesus Christ's teachings are constant and relevant through all eras.

However, before we explore strategies and tools, we need to pause and recognize a vital truth: the urgency of this moment. Every generation has faced its own challenges, but for Gen Z and Gen Alpha, the stakes seem higher than ever. Truths are often seen as relative, loneliness has become widespread, and anxiety and depression are at record levels. If we do not reach this generation now, they risk being overwhelmed by many voices competing for their attention—voices that offer fleeting satisfaction but leave behind a more bottomless emptiness.

Yet, amid this chaos, we carry the only message that can truly transform. The Gospel is not just another opinion; it is the voice that brings life, hope, and purpose.

That voice, the voice of the gospel, changed my life forever at seventeen. My passion for this stems from my experience with leaders who believe in the next generation and can profoundly influence a young person's life. Though it may seem small at first, like planting a bamboo seed, that seed grew into something tall and beautiful over time with prayer and intentional discipleship.

You—pastors, parents, and leaders—are on the frontlines of this mission. Let my story serve as a reminder of the powerful impact a mentor, pastor, or role model can have, especially one who loves Christ and brings others closer to Him.

As I write this, I am filled with gratitude for those who believed in me when I struggled to believe in myself, recognizing my potential even when I felt lost. My parents played a vital role in my salvation. My college football coaches, filled with intensity and passion, exemplified a life that honored God. My first youth pastor, Jose, showed me that being a Christian is serious yet also the most fun, and that laughter is essential. My Pastor now, Pastor Alex Sagot, with whom I have served both during his time as Youth Pastor and now, deepened my understanding of preaching to a lost generation with passion. The list of Godly mentors continues, and their influence mattered then—and it still inspires me today.

FROM RELUCTANT TEEN TO YOUTH PASTOR

Now, fast-forward to today, and never in a million years did I think I would be a pastor, much less a Youth Pastor. Teenage Phil would have laughed (or swore) at the very suggestion. But here I am, leading students, shepherding families, and authoring this book.

My story of salvation starts with a lost, angry, selfish seventeen-year-old who is trying to balance the chaos of his parents' divorce and a burden of shame from poor choices. At that moment, my life felt like a blindfolded circus act—juggling sins, relationships, and mistakes but constantly dropping the ball.

Then I was forced to go to a Youth Camp for a week in the middle of nowhere, Florida. Away from my family, friends, and the environment that was leading me to sin. Like most young people, I did not want to be there. As a caring and loving parent, my mother made sure I attended. AKA I was forced to go. Which is a great parenting tip: force your kids to go to youth camp. I was imagining all the "cool" things I could have been doing instead—drinking, partying, chasing validation all summer. But one night at camp, something happened. I do not even remember what the pastor said. I recall the moment the Gospel was presented, and the invitation was extended. My legs seemed to move on their own, and before I knew it, I was at the altar. The Lord was calling to me.

I did not know much about Jesus, but I knew I had to say "yes." That moment did not turn me into an angel overnight, but it changed my eternity. It gave my life meaning. Over time, God worked on me—transforming me from a rowdy teenager notorious for stirring up trouble at youth camp to someone called to shepherd others. You cannot tell me God does not have a sense of humor.

Pastor, parent, or leader, if you are reading this and feel discouraged about a student or child who seems "too far gone," remember that no one is beyond the reach of Christ's love.

Let us be honest: being in youth ministry or parenting a teenager today is tough. As a Youth Pastor, it used to be that our key role was to warn kids about sex, drugs, and alcohol. Now, we are handling conversations about gender identity, mental health, social justice, politics, and the growing list of challenges they face. Some days, it can feel overwhelming. Likewise, being a parent involves careful communication. The depth of discussions we need to have with our children, because of the importance of these topics that demand responses, can be pretty daunting.

Makes you wonder: "Is what I am doing even working? Do any of these students care? Am I wasting my time?"

I have asked myself these questions more times than I can count. Sometimes, I wish I could be a youth pastor in another era—like the '90s, when life seemed simpler, and ministry felt more straightforward. Just imagine taking our small group to a Blockbuster to hang out, play video games, and enjoy lots of candy—a perfect way to connect with any middle school boy. Our youth ministry would have thrived.

Think about the prices of fast food back then. As a '90s kid, I remember going to McDonald's on Wednesdays for 49-cent hamburgers and 79-cent cheeseburgers. Imagine doing outreach for students and treating them to burgers without worrying about scraping by for a month to cover the cost. Nowadays, McDonald's can sometimes feel like dining at a Michelin-starred restaurant.

What I have come to grips with is this: We do not need to daydream about the past because today's reality is right in front of us, and unfortunately, we cannot travel back in time.

A quote from The Lord of the Rings comes to mind when Frodo laments the weight of his journey: "I wish it not happened in my time," said Frodo. "So do I," said Gandalf, "and so do all who live to see such times. But that is not for them to decide. All we have to decide is what to do with the time that is given us."[3]

We find a similar tension in Esther 4:14 ESV "For if you keep silent at this time, relief and deliverance will rise for the Jews from another place, but you and your father's house will perish. And who knows whether you have not come to the kingdom for such a time as this?"

Esther, an orphan in Babylonian exile, rises from obscurity to prominence when she catches the eye of the king of Persia during a dysfunctional beauty pageant. As her story unfolds, we see both Esther and her cousin Mordecai, faithful Jews, find favor with the king. Tension builds when Haman, a descendant of the Canaanites, takes offense at Mordecai's refusal to bow to him. Consumed by pride and vengeance, Haman manipulates the king into signing a decree to annihilate all the Jews in Persia.

Suddenly, Esther becomes the Jews' only hope. Mordecai devises a daring plan: Esther must reveal her Jewish identity and plead with the king to save her people. Although God is never explicitly mentioned in the book of Esther, His hand is clearly at work, guiding events behind the scenes.

Similarly, as we consider the cultural chaos surrounding today's young people, it is easy to wonder, where is God in all of this? But the story of Esther reminds us that even when we cannot see Him, God is still at work. Mordecai recognized that Esther's rise to the throne was no accident. He urged her to have the courage and wisdom to understand her God-given purpose and fulfill it. The same principle applies to us today. Wherever God has placed us—whether in a classroom, a youth group, or a church—He has done so for a reason. It is our responsibility to step into that purpose with faith and boldness.

Charles Spurgeon puts it beautifully: "You have been wishing for another position where you could do something for Jesus: do not wish anything of the kind but serve him where you are."[4]

What if, instead of longing for simpler times, we embraced this moment as the greatest opportunity for student ministry? What if, instead of fearing for our children's future, we began training them in the ways of the Lord now? Yes, the opposition is fierce, but so is the potential for revival. We were born for this moment. This is our time.

I am not presenting myself as an authority with all the answers, nor do I lead the most well-known youth group or oversee a high-profile ministry. However, my experiences, including many mistakes, have provided valuable lessons. By sharing these insights, I aim to help others in my position avoid making the same mistakes and make more effective use of their time. My goal is to ensure that every decision, program, and interaction with young people is intentional and impactful, thereby contributing positively to a generation facing significant challenges if we do not act purposefully.

Whether you are a youth pastor in the trenches, a parent desperate to understand your child, or a volunteer wondering if your late nights and long hours make any difference, this book is for you.

The journey will not be easy, but the stakes are too high to give up. The young people we are fighting for are worth it. Let us get to work.

THE KIDS ARE NOT ALRIGHT

Imagine a teenager scrolling through their phone late at night. Hundreds of followers surround them online, yet they feel deeply alone. They are searching for purpose, but the endless stream of content leaves them overwhelmed and anxious.

This is the reality of Gen Z and Gen Alpha, two generations growing up in a world more connected—and yet more isolated—than ever before. They are curious about spirituality, but they are unsure where to find answers. They are yearning for meaning, but the noise of culture drowns out the voice of truth.

Let us take a moment to understand who these young people are, the challenges they face, and why the Church must rise to the occasion. Because if we do not act now, we risk losing them—not just to culture but to hopelessness.

Founding Pastor of Church of the Highlands, Chris Hodges, emphasizes the importance of data for improving his church in his Grow Leader Podcast, saying, "Numbers are an indicator of health." He asks, "Do we know our numbers?" He illustrates this by comparing it to a medical emergency—if a paramedic arrives on the scene, the first thing they do is check vital signs, such as heart rate, temperature, and blood pressure. Their role is to assess the seriousness of the situation and understand how well we are doing.[5]

Similarly, do we genuinely understand how Generation Z and Generation Alpha are faring in terms of their mental health, social life, and faith? Are we truly informed? This is not about making estimates based on a few students who may be acting up in service or solely relying on social media for insights into young people. Have we conducted thorough research using available resources to gauge the well-being of these generations? This understanding is critical for us to formulate an effective plan of action to address their needs.

Numbers do not lie. I want to present some numbers and data that can help us gauge the pulse of the generation we are trying to lead and give you an idea of what we are dealing with.

WHO ARE GEN Z AND ALPHA?

Gen Z (born 1997–2012): This group includes middle schoolers, high schoolers, and young adults. They are the first digital natives, growing up with smartphones, social media, and instant access to information.

Gen Alpha (born 2013–2025): The youngest generation, still in elementary and middle school, who are growing up in the shadow of a pandemic and rapid cultural shifts.

Both generations are marked by:

Constant Connectivity: They have never known a world without Wi-Fi or smartphones.

Heightened Awareness: Social issues, mental health, and global crises are part of their everyday vocabulary.

Search for Authenticity: They value transparency and are quick to spot hypocrisy.

According to recent studies, Gen Z shows a significantly lower rate of religious affiliation compared to earlier generations, with a sizable part identifying as religiously unaffiliated, atheist, or agnostic. At the same time, Gen Alpha, still young, appears to hold more positive views on religion, often valuing the social aspects of faith and aligning with the idea of helping others. However, their specific beliefs are still developing and heavily influenced by their family environment.

THE EMOTIONAL AND SPIRITUAL STATE
OF THE NEXT GENERATION

60% of Christian youth leave the Church after high school graduation. This is not just a number; it is a sobering reminder of how many young people are abandoning their faith.[6]

69% of teens express curiosity about the Bible, and 67% perceive it as relevant to their lives. The hunger for truth is there, but curiosity alone is not enough. They need guidance to move from curiosity to commitment. 93% of students believe it is their responsibility to share their faith, but 85% wish they were better equipped to do so.[7]

The last statistic highlights both their potential as Gospel carriers and the Church's need to equip them effectively.

Beyond the statistics lies a generation in pain: Loneliness is an Epidemic: social media connects them, but does not satisfy their more profound need for belonging. Gen Z and Alpha are hyperconnected online yet spiritually disconnected.

We are raising a generation that knows how to connect to Wi-Fi but struggles to connect with purpose.

Mental Health Struggles Are Unprecedented: Anxiety, depression, and suicidal ideation are at all-time highs for teens.

Spiritual Confusion Is Rampant: Many are open to faith conversations, but they are inundated with conflicting worldviews that make truth seem relative and subjective.

Curiosity about Jesus is widespread in this generation. Teens in the US are far more intrigued than their global peers, with 77% being at least motivated to keep learning about Jesus throughout their lives. (The Open Generation)[8]

What does all this mean? Students are curious but lack discipleship to grow. Curiosity alone will not anchor them. It is our role to turn that curiosity into conviction and discipleship.

Our methods must evolve to reach them, but the message of the Gospel is still unchanged.

The truth is that many youth leaders and parents feel under-equipped to answer the deep questions that Generation Z and Generation Alpha are asking. One of the reasons I felt compelled to draft this book was the countless conversations I have had with youth leaders and parents who repeatedly asked how to help their students struggling with depression. I have also had parents ask that I sit down with their children to teach them about the Bible because they felt ill-equipped to do so themselves. These examples reflect a concerning lack of confidence in making a meaningful impact on the lives of these students.

Intimidation can stem from the overwhelming amount of data revealing the challenges we face with the next generation. However, despite the many obstacles, it is essential to recognize that these challenges also present many opportunities for the gospel to spread rapidly.

Now back to the data. I am not sure if you read that first statistic quickly or not, but it is worth restating: 60% of students who grow up in the Church are leaving after high school.

This is not just a trend; it is a wake-up call. If we do not engage with young people today with the Gospel now, we risk losing them to a world that offers connection but no true belonging.

The good news? 69% of students are curious about the Bible, and 67% believe it is relevant to their lives. The grave news? Most of them are not being discipled in a way that translates curiosity into life transformation. They are familiar with the Bible, but they often struggle to apply its teachings in their daily lives.[9]

Let me challenge you with this thought: What is the point of having students curious about faith if we do not give them the tools to share it? 85% of students wish they were better at sharing their faith, yet many feel unprepared. It is on us to change that. We will discuss this more in later chapters. [10]

The data paints a bleak picture, but it also reveals an opportunity for improvement. This generation is hungry for truth, purpose, and belonging—three things the Church is uniquely equipped to offer. But we must do more than sit back and hope they will walk through our doors.

We need to address their questions: Who am I? Why am I here? Where do I belong? These are the questions they are asking, and the Church must have answers that are biblically grounded and culturally relevant. We must model authenticity: Gen Z and Alpha value transparency. They do not want perfect leaders; they want real ones. We must be bold in discipleship: the goal is not just to keep them in the church, but to disciple them into lifelong followers of Christ. This means prioritizing relationships, mentorship, and equipping them to live out their faith.

A MOMENT OF DECISION

The next generation is at a crossroads, and so are we. Will we rise to the challenge of reaching them, or will we let them drift away?

George Barna once said, "In the race to a child's heart, the first one there wins." The question is not whether they will be influenced—it is who will affect them.[11]

> "George Barna once said, 'In the race to a child's heart, the first one there wins.' The question is not whether they will be influenced—it is who will affect them."

The good news is that it is not too late. The Church has the power, the resources, and the message of hope they need. But we must act now because the kids are not all right. And they are counting on us to show them the way.

Before we delve into the heart of this book, I would like to share a framework that will guide our discussion. These are not just catchy ideas—they are the pillars that will help us lead effectively and reach the next generation for Christ.

This mission is not a sprint; it is a marathon. And like any marathon, you need the proper foundation to keep going when the road gets tough. For me, that foundation boils down to three key areas: Character, Community, and Culture.

Part 1: Character—It Starts with Us

If we want to influence the next generation, we must let God shape our character first. As we have discussed already students are drawn to authenticity. They do not expect us to be perfect, but they do expect us to be authentic.

Character is not just about avoiding mistakes; it is about letting God refine us through the highs and the lows. It is about living a life that aligns with what we teach and being willing to grow along the way.

This first section will examine what it means to lead from a place of integrity and humility. You cannot pour into others if you are running empty, so we will discuss how to let God fill you up so you can pour into the next generation.

Part 2: Community—The Antidote to Loneliness

Let us face it: loneliness is everywhere, and young people feel it most. They are navigating a more connected world than ever, leaving them feeling unseen and unheard.

The Church has a unique opportunity to step in and provide the belonging students crave. However, building a community is not just about getting students to show up; it is about helping them feel at home. It is about creating spaces where they can experience the love of Christ through authentic relationships.

In Part 2, we will focus on how to foster that sense of belonging. From building relationships to creating opportunities for students to participate in the church's life, we will discuss how to show them that they do not have to walk this journey alone.

Part 3: Culture—What We Do Matters

Culture is not what you say, it is what you consistently do. It is the atmosphere you create in your church, ministry, and family.

In today's world, culture can either attract or repel young people. The good news is that we can create a culture that makes them want to stay—not because we water down the truth but because we make it irresistible.

In Part 3, we will get practical. We will cover strategies to create a church culture that is engaging, welcoming, and centered on discipleship. We will talk about building worship experiences that connect, empowering young leaders to serve, and fostering a spirit of unity that draws students closer to Jesus.

A ROADMAP FOR WHAT IS AHEAD

These three parts—Character, Community, and Culture—are concepts and pathways. Each build on the other, creating an integrated approach to reaching Gen Z and Gen Alpha.

As we read this book, I want you to know that this journey is not just about strategies or quick fixes. It is about transformation—starting with us and extending to the young people we are called to lead.

So here is my challenge: What will you do with the time you have been given? Will you step into this moment with courage, faith, and a willingness to grow? The future of the Church is being shaped right now, and together, we can help the next generation step into their God-given purpose.

Let us get started.

PART 1

CHARACTER

"The best thing you bring to leadership is
your own transformed soul. Your life is your
message, not just your sermon or podcast."

— JOHN MARK COMER, 12

"A week after my 18th birthday, I turned to weed to fill the void… but Jesus met me there and flipped everything." – Daniel

"Freshman year, I almost gave up trying to please everyone. God's presence in my room one night reminded me who I really am." – Jenny

"God broke off timidity in me. I went from being afraid to speak up to leading and praying boldly for others." – Grace

Chapter 1

The Power of a Self-Aware Leader

"People may be right in their own eyes, but the Lord examines their hearts." Proverbs 21:2

Big Idea: You cannot grow if you do not know. Leaders who lack self-awareness will eventually lose the very people they were called to lead.

WHAT I COULD NOT SEE

Most leaders do not fail because they do not care. They fail because they do not see what they are missing.

Self-awareness is not about insecurity or self-obsession. It is about humility. And without it, even well-intentioned leaders can slowly drift away from the very people God has called them to serve.

Early in my ministry journey, I served as a small group leader for the senior boys in our youth ministry. I loved it. I wanted to be great at it. I thought I was doing well—until someone I trusted pulled me aside and showed me what I could not see.

At the time, our youth pastor (now my lead pastor), Pastor Alex Sagot, pulled me aside one Friday night after our youth service. He affirmed me first—told me he believed in my leadership. But then he said something that changed everything.

He said, "Phil, you're spending all your time trying to chase the guys who aren't showing up… but what about the ones who are?"

He was right. I was so focused on pursuing the students who had ghosted on Friday nights that I unintentionally neglected the ones who came eager, hungry, and ready to be discipled.

That moment taught me something I could not unlearn when leaders lack self-awareness, they do not just mismanage their energy — they unintentionally wound the faithful.

I did not see it. I could not see it. I lacked self-awareness. But because someone I trusted saw it and loved me enough to say it, I was able to shift. I grew. As a result, I became a better leader.

That moment taught me something that is stuck with me ever since: Your greatest leadership ceiling might not be your talent... but your ability to see yourself clearly.

THE LEADERSHIP BLIND SPOT

Every leader has blind spots. It is not a matter of if—it is just a matter of when they will show up and whether you will allow God (and others) to reveal them before they hurt the people you are trying to lead.

We live in a culture obsessed with self-expression, but allergic to self-examination. We teach students to post their truth, share their vibe, and curate their identity—but how often do we slow down long enough to ask: "What's really going on inside of me?"

As leaders, we cannot afford to live unaware. Why? Because students are watching. They might not have the words to explain it, but they can feel when something is off in our spirit. They can sense when we are reacting out of insecurity or leading out of unhealed wounds

Self-awareness does not mean you see everything clearly it means you are willing to be shown.

WHO ARE YOU BECOMING?

All that to say that the older I get, the less I focus on what I do and the more I care about who I am becoming. As leaders, we often place value on our accomplishments—our "doing." However, the actual, lasting impact flows not from what we do, but from who we are.

This shift requires something often overlooked in leadership: self-awareness. It is the ability to understand who we are, how we behave, and how we are perceived by others—all while aligning our lives with God's truth. In a world that celebrates charisma over character, self-awareness is one of the most essential tools for any leader.

For Gen Z and Gen Alpha, who crave authenticity and connection, self-awareness in leadership is not optional—it is nonnegotiable. They do not just want to hear about Jesus; they want to see Him reflected in the lives of those leading them.

WHAT IS SELF AWARENESS?

Psychologists Shelley Duval and Robert Wicklund define self-awareness as the ability to focus on oneself and assess how one's actions, thoughts, or emotions align with one's internal standards.[13] For Christians, this means asking: Am I living in alignment with who I am in Christ?

Self-awareness forces us to wrestle with deep, often uncomfortable questions:

- Why am I defensive?

- Why do I lose my temper so easily?

- Why can't I believe that God truly loves me?

Without self-awareness, we risk being blind to the impact we have on others. Robert Cheong explains: "A lack of self-awareness hinders our ability to love and lead others. Without understanding how we struggle to love God and others, we will not seek Christ to change the way we love."

For the next generation, leaders who lack self-awareness become barriers to faith rather than bridges to Christ.

WHY WE NEED SELF AWARE LEADERS

Here is the main villain on your journey to becoming a self-aware leader. Are you ready? It might shock you. Here it is. Your perception. That is right, your perception of who I am versus others' experience of who I am can be far apart.

> **"If we do not see and understand how we struggle to love God and others, we will not seek Christ to change the way we love."**

In other words, A lack of self-awareness hinders our awareness of the hearts and lives of others, which affects how we love and lead those around us. If we do not see and understand how we struggle to love God and others, we will not seek Christ to change the way we love.

If we are not careful, instead of walking in self-awareness, we will be walking around in self-denial.

We will refuse to face reality; we will live in a fantasy world; we will become incredibly naïve or typically either grossly overestimate or underestimate our gifts and talents, as well as what genuinely accounts for who we are and what they do.

Steve Jobs was famous for many things. The iPod and iPhone, to name a few. Now these items made him famous around the world, but his reality distortion field (RDF) made him famous among his coworkers. Jobs's ability to convince himself and others around him to believe anything with a mix of charm, charisma, bravado, hyperbole, marketing, appeasement, and persistence. It was said to distort his co-workers' sense of proportion and scales of difficulties and to make them believe that whatever impossible task he had at hand was possible. But the reality was he was manipulative, disrespectful, and could never be told he was wrong. He created another world where only Steve Jobs was the hero.[14]

Truthfully, he achieved a great deal using his RDF, but at the expense of his character. Our character, which is supposed to resemble Christ, could be jeopardized if we create our own "RDF" and close ourselves off to any help or awareness that can save us.

Dr. Tasha Eurich spent more than 10 years surveying people about their levels of self-awareness. She has found that while 95% of study participants think they are self-aware, only about 10% to 15% of them are fully self-aware.[15]

If authenticity is something this generation yearns for in their leaders, then we cannot take this lightly.

Our young people, sadly, are growing up in a world saturated with fake personas and curated social media feeds. They have become experts at spotting inauthenticity. If they sense that their leaders are disconnected from their own struggles or putting up a façade, they will disengage.

Here's why self-aware leadership matters for these generations: They value authenticity. I believe young people do not expect perfection, but they demand honesty. When a leader is self-aware, they model what it looks like to follow Jesus with humility and transparency. This opens the door for students to trust them.

When someone becomes a leader or gains influence, their actions are closely scrutinized. This is also evident in parenting. Children learn by seeing their parents' behavior, such as patience, self-control, and the process of making amends. It is essential to consider what others perceive in our actions, including the views of students.

What are people seeing from your life? What are students seeing out of you? What are your children learning from you as they watch your life?

These generations do not just listen to what you say, they watch how you live. When they see leaders who admit their weaknesses and strive to grow, they are more likely to embrace the same journey in their own lives.

"These generations do not just listen to what you say, they watch how you live."

A self-aware leader shows students and others how to process failure through the lens of grace. When leaders acknowledge their mistakes and seek forgiveness, they teach the next generation how to rely on Christ rather than hiding their struggles.

THE SELF-AWARE LEADER: 3 MARKS

In his book *Leveling Up,* Ryan Leak outlines three characteristics of a self-aware leader:

1. They Know Their Strengths

Self-aware leaders confidently use their gifts to bless and serve, without succumbing to false humility. They show what it looks like to steward God-given talents for His glory.

2. They Acknowledge Their Weaknesses

Humility enables self-aware leaders to acknowledge their limitations and demonstrate their dependence on God. This teaches students that it is okay not to have all the answers and to lean on God's strength.

3. They Understand Their Impact on Others

Self-aware leaders actively seek feedback and are willing to change. This fosters an environment of empathy and safety, showing students how to listen, grow, and prioritize relationships.[16]

HOW SELF AWARENESS BUILDS TRUST AND CONNECTION

The next generation is seeking leaders who not only preach the Gospel but also embody it. Here's how self-awareness bridges the gap:

It Creates Relational Safety. When leaders are open about their journey, students feel safe sharing their own struggles. These builds trust and foster authentic discipleship.

It Breaks Down Barriers. A lack of self-awareness can create walls between leaders and students. But when leaders acknowledge their blind spots and work to grow, it breaks down those barriers and opens the door for connection.

It Inspires Vulnerability. Vulnerability is contagious. When leaders are vulnerable, it allows students to do the same, creating a culture of honesty and healing.

At the core of self-awareness is the desire to become more like Christ. Jesus exemplified humility, courage, and love—qualities that are difficult to cultivate without the willingness to see ourselves honestly. Let us make it our mission to live each day with humility, modeling the example set in Philippians 2:5-8 (NLT): 5 You must have the same attitude that Christ Jesus had. 6 Though he was God, he did not think of equality with God as something to cling to.7 Instead, he gave up his divine privileges; he took the humble position of a slave and was born as a human being. When he appeared in human form, 8 he humbled himself in obedience to God and died a criminal's death on a cross.

When it comes to looking more like Jesus, Pastor and Author John Mark Comer shares in his book, Practicing the Way, "the single most important question is, are we becoming more loving? Not are we becoming more biblically educated? Or practicing more spiritual disciplines? Or more involved in Church? Those are all good things, but not the most important thing." [17]

John Mark goes on to say that to test the progress of our journey, becoming more like Christ, we should test the quality of our close relationships.

He challenges us by asking the question, "Are you growing in love, not just for your friends and family, but for your enemies? By loving, I mean becoming more like Christ and loving the way he did when he laid his life down for us.

The biggest hurdle in living out the humility of Jesus is the belief that promotion is in our hands rather than in God's. Let me clarify, showing up late to work every day will not bring you closer to a promotion at your job. However, experiencing supernatural influence and favor—opening doors not just in your career but also in your relationships—comes only from heaven.

The stress of trying to elevate ourselves using every fiber of our being can be alleviated when our trust in Christ is stronger than our pride in ourselves. Jesus himself tells us in Matthew 23:11-12 (ESV): "The greatest among you shall be your servant. Whoever exalts himself will be humbled, and whoever humbles himself will be exalted."

A self-aware leader gives a living example of what it means to follow Jesus authentically. When they see us acknowledge our weaknesses, seek forgiveness, and rely on God, the next generation can learn to do the same.

Self-awareness is not about perfection; it is about alignment. When we align our hearts with God's truth and open ourselves to His refining work, we become the kind of leaders who inspire the next generation to walk boldly with Christ.

PRACTICAL STEPS TO GROW IN SELF AWARENESS

Growing in self-awareness is not easy, but it is worth it. Here are some steps to get started:

Ask for Honest Feedback

Start with those who know you best. Use questions like:

- What is it like to be led by me?
- What is it like to be my friend?
- What is it like to serve with me?

Reflect with Scripture and Prayer

Psalm 139:23-24 says, "Search me, God, and know my heart… See if there is any offensive way in me." Make this your prayer as you invite God to reveal areas for growth.

Practice Non-Defensive Listening

When someone gives feedback, resist the urge to explain or justify yourself. Instead, thank them and reflect on what they have said. The irony of asking for feedback is when we receive it, we push against it. Let us be leaders that when we ask for help or assign men and woman of God to call us out, we do not resist in defiance but respond with gratitude and humility.

> **"Let us be leaders that when we ask for help or assign men and woman of God to call us out, we do not resist in defiance but respond with gratitude and humility."**

Self-aware leaders do not lead from perfection they lead from humility. They invite correction, remain teachable, and refuse to confuse activity with fruitfulness. If we want to lead the next generation well, it must start here: with an honest look at our hearts and a willingness to grow. Because leaders who are willing to be examined by God are the ones He trusts to shape others.

REFLECTION QUESTIONS

What blind spots has God been trying to highlight recently?

Who has permission to speak honestly in my life – and do I listen?

How does pride or insecurity distort the way I see myself?

Where do I tend to overestimate my leadership strengths?

———————

Chapter 2

The Addiction of Applause

"Be careful not to practice your righteousness in front of others to be seen by them. If you do, you will have no reward from your Father in heaven." Matthew 6:1

Big Idea: You cannot lead the next generation if you need their approval more than God's affirmation.

APPLAUSE THAT FADES

Every leader wants to be encouraged. That is not the problem.

The problem begins when affirmation becomes fuel and silence feels like failure.

In a world of likes, shares, numbers, and metrics, it is easy to confuse visibility with faithfulness. And if we are not careful, we can begin leading for applause instead of obedience.

Actress and singer Judy Garland was widely recognized for her work, particularly for her iconic role in the classic film The Wizard of Oz. She was a prominent star during her career. Unfortunately, she passed away at the age of 47. At the time of her death, the New York Times published an article that I believe relates to all of us. This is an excerpt from the article.

"LONDON, June 22- Judy Garland, whose successes on stage and screen were later overshadowed by the pathos of her personal life, was found dead in her home here today. Miss Garland's personal life often seemed a fruitless search for the happiness promised in "Over the Rainbow," the song she made famous in the movie "The Wizard of Oz." Her father died

when she was 12 years old; the pressures of adolescent stardom sent her to a psychiatrist at the age of 18; she was married five times; she was frequently ill; her singing voice faltered, and she suffered from the effects of drugs she once said were prescribed either to invigorate or tranquilize her. Judy Garland's career was marked by a compulsive quality that displayed itself even during her first performance at the age of 30 months at the New Grand Theater in Grand Rapids, Minn. Here, the story is told, she was singing "Jingle Bells" at a Christmas program. She responded so favorably to the footlights that her father was forced to remove her after she repeated the song seven times. The other side of the compulsively vibrant, exhausting performances that were her stage hallmark was an unquenchable need for her audiences to respond with acclaim and affection. And often they did, screaming, "We love you, Judy- we love you."

Towards the end of her life, she was quoted as saying, "In the silence of night I have often wished for just a few words of love from one man, rather than the applause of thousands of people."[18]

Her story feels painfully familiar—not because we all dream of standing on Broadway stages, but because we all know the pull of human approval. We have felt the rush when someone praises our work or notices our effort. But we have also felt the hollowness that comes when that applause fades.

For those of us in ministry and in life, the applause of others can easily become an idol. We start by serving God, but somewhere along the way, the approval of people creeps in, and our motives shift. Why do we serve? Is it to make Jesus known, or is it to make ourselves known?

In a culture obsessed with likes, shares, and follows, the addiction to applause is not just a temptation—it is a battle for the soul. And if we, as leaders, fall into this trap, how can we model authentic faith for the next generation?

FROM FILM ROW TO FRONT ROW

Before ministry, there was football.

I played the game from little league through college, and I loved it—but more than that, I needed it. Not just the wins or the workouts, but the spotlight. I needed to be seen. I worked hard to pop on film, win every drill, and make plays that would catch the coach's attention. Because I knew that if I did not get noticed, I would not get to play. If I had not played, I felt worthless.

Sitting on the bench was a different kind of pain, especially when you are watching someone in your position who you do not believe is better than you.

That mindset did not remain confined to the field; it carried over into my ministry. For many of us, this is also a common reality. Our flesh can plant a toxic thought in our minds that says, "If I don't get noticed, I won't get to play." Or "If the pastor doesn't see me picking up trash, I might miss my chance to preach."

I did not realize it at first, but somewhere along the way, I stopped finding joy in serving and started obsessing over being seen. I compared myself to other leaders. I questioned my calling. My self-worth was tied to who clapped, who reposted, who noticed. And the worst part? It started affecting everything—my marriage, my friendships, even my preaching.

It is like I was a fish on a hook—the applause felt good at first… but it was killing me.

So, I did the only thing I could do I went back to the beginning.

Back to when I first walked into Calvary. I was not the youth pastor. I was not even on the radar. I was just the guy picking up trash and cleaning toilets. And I loved it. Why? Because I believed God saw me—and that was enough.

Back then, I did not seek to be known. I served because I was known by Him. And that was all I needed.

I was trained by the sacred arts of stacking chairs (IYKYK), and it kept me grounded. There was no ladder to climb—just joy in doing whatever needed to be done.

Now, 14 years into youth ministry, I still must remind myself: applause fades, but obedience lasts.

If we do not keep our motives in check, we will start building platforms for ourselves instead of altars for God. In other words, if we do not deal with our need to be seen, we will never be free to serve.

THE SUBTLE TRAP OF APPROVAL

Now, approval is not inherently bad, and applause itself is not dangerous dependence on it is. From an early age, we are wired to seek affirmation—from parents, teachers, and peers. But when the need for validation becomes the driving force behind our actions, it distorts our purpose.

This is the danger Jesus addressed in Matthew 6. He warned against practicing righteousness "to be seen by others." The Pharisees of His day were not just following the law—they were performing it, ensuring their acts of piety were as public as possible. Their reward? The applause of people, but nothing more.

In ministry, it is easy to justify actions with spiritual language. We say we are "building the Kingdom" or "doing it for God's glory," but deep down, are we seeking something else? The applause of others can quietly replace the approval of God, and when that happens, our ministry becomes more about us than Him.

Jesus does not just care about what we do; He cares about why we do it. The Sermon on the Mount was not just a list of commands—it was a call to examine the heart. Our bible warns

"Jesus does not just care about what we do; He cares about why we do it."

us of the dangers that come from using our hearts as a compass to find true satisfaction.

We see this in Jeremiah 17:9-10 ESV 9 The heart is deceitful above all things, and desperately sick; who can understand it? 10 "I the Lord search the heart and test the mind, to give every man according to his ways, according to the fruit of his deeds."

We cannot make something that is already corrupt more corrupt. Allow the Lord to examine your heart and to rearrange or remove any sin that is cancerous to your spirit.

The road to cleansing your heart starts with a question every leader must wrestle with: Does this glorify God, or does this glorify me?

THE CHAINS OF HYPOCRISY

The word "hypocrite" comes from the Greek word for an actor—someone who wears a mask and performs for an audience. In ministry or at work, it is dangerously easy to slip into this role. We post photos of packed rooms, share the highlights of our sermons, and wait for the affirming comments to roll in.

But beneath the surface, the addiction to applause leaves us hollow. Instead of serving God authentically, we become performers—chasing likes, shares, and praise.

James 5:16 NIV tells us, 16 Therefore confess your sins to each other and pray for each other so that you may be healed. The prayer of a righteous person is powerful and effective.

James calls us to do something radically different: confession. True freedom begins when we drop the mask and allow ourselves to be fully seen—first by God, then by others.

Whatever stays hidden will always stay hurt. True freedom is walking out of your door every day, having peace that you know who you are in

"Whatever stays hidden will always stay hurt."

Christ Jesus. You do not have to pretend or hide behind a persona. Sure, there will always be aspects of ourselves that we dislike, but the core of who we are and who God has created us to be can bring us joy.

Many of our young people walk around wearing masks to impress their peers, whether in class or online. Until they are taught and shown the beauty of confession, they will stay a slave to attention.

Charles Spurgeon once said, "Keep the thing so secret that even you yourself are hardly aware that you are doing anything at all praiseworthy. Let God be present, and you will have enough of an audience."[19]

This is the antidote to the addiction of applause: living for the approval of one. When our motives are rooted in God's pleasure, we experience freedom. We no longer need to prove ourselves or seek validation from others.

But this is not just about us—it is about the next generation.

There is an interesting passage in Ecclesiastes 9:14-15 that I want us to examine, which I believe will challenge us.

14 There was once a small city with only a few inhabitants. A powerful king came against it, surrounded it, and built huge siege works against it. 15 Now, in that city lived a poor but wise man, and he saved the city by his wisdom. However, nobody remembered that poor man.

Here we see a city in trouble. A poor, wise man saves the city, yet nobody remembers him. This last verse can feel quite haunting. How could a man who saved a city under attack be forgotten? Did the people not appreciate his sacrifice? Did they belittle his efforts? Why was he not remembered when he deserved recognition?

However, these are not the right questions to ask. There is a more profound message that Solomon is trying to convey. The questions Solomon presents are:

- Would you still save a city if nobody knew it was you?

- Would you act even if you never received credit for it?

- Would you do something significant even if you weren't recognized for it?

St. John Chrysostom shares a sobering thought: "If you knew how quickly people would forget you after your death, you would not seek in your life to please anyone but God". [20]

ALL EYES ON US

Gen Z and Alpha are growing up in a world where approval is a form of currency. Social media platforms are built on metrics that quantify worth through likes, comments, and followers. These generations are constantly told their value is tied to their performance or popularity.

As leaders, we have the opportunity—and responsibility—to model something different. The hard truth that often goes unmentioned when you become a Christian and a leader is that the moment you say yes to Jesus and accept His call, everyone around you starts watching your every move. People want to see if the Jesus you claim to follow is real, and your life becomes the evidence of that truth. This is especially true for students who are looking for someone to guide them. To lead the way.

Let us provide young people with real-life examples of vulnerability. They do not want perfect leaders; they want leaders who are real. No masks, just raw honesty. They are seeking individuals who live authentically, acknowledge their struggles, and prioritize God's approval over human applause.

Through our example of practicing confession and being honest about our struggles, we show them what absolute freedom looks like. When young people see leaders serving without pretense or performance, it shows them what it means to live free from the pressures of performance.

What is beautiful about being vulnerable is that it can be empowering for the person who is a witness to it. We can empower our young people and teach them that their worth is not tied to their achievements but to their identity in Christ. Encourage them to serve out of love for God, not out of a desire for recognition.

We can show them that there is more to life than followers, likes, viewers, trophies, and more. Nothing wrong with working to achieve success but we can teach that real success is living everyday knowing you are already loved by Jesus and that love did not come because of anything they did but only from all that he did for us.

THE AUDIENCE OF ONE

A world-renowned violinist once gave a performance of a lifetime. The crowd erupted into a standing ovation, but the musician walked off the stage in tears. When asked why, he replied, "If my father, my teacher, doesn't stand, it doesn't matter what anyone else does."

As leaders, only one applause truly matters: the applause of our Heavenly Father. His approval is not based on our performance but on our faithfulness. When we align our motives with His will, we experience the freedom to lead authentically, love wholeheartedly, and serve with integrity.

Applause is a poor compass it always points toward what is popular, not what is right.[21]

For the next generation, this is not just a lesson it is a lifeline. Let us show them what it means to live for the audience of one, so they, too, can experience the joy of serving a God who sees and rewards what is done in secret.

Psalm 118:8 reminds us: "It is better to take refuge in the Lord than to trust in man."

May we lead for His glory, not our own—and in doing so, inspire the next generation to do the same.

REMEMBER THE BEGINNING

When I feel the pull of applause again, I go back to where it all started. Before the mic. Before the ministry title. Just a young leader who loved Jesus, stacked chairs, cleaned bathrooms, and believed God saw it all. That is what set me free. And that is what keeps me going. You do not need to be famous. You just need to be faithful. We will expound on the power of remembering in a later chapter but for now let make it our mission to live for the audience of one!

Leaders who are addicted to applause will always be exhausted. But leaders who are anchored in obedience are free. Free to serve when no one notices. Free to stay when growth feels slow. Free to trust that God sees what others do not. If we want to lead the next generation with integrity, we must learn to celebrate faithfulness even when it goes unrecognized.

REFLECTION QUESTIONS

What triggers your desire for recognition or approval?

Are there moments where you have chosen applause over obedience?

What spiritual disciplines (prayer, solitude, fasting) help you stay grounded?

When was the last time you served in a way that no one saw but God?

Chapter 3

Submission Helps the Mission

"Obey your leaders and submit to them, for they are keeping watch over your souls, as those who will have to give an account." Hebrews 13:17

Big Idea: Submission is not weakness-it is the spiritual posture that unlocks alignment, authority, and blessing.

THE SWORD OF OUR WILL

For many leaders, the word submission does not bring clarity it brings tension. It reminds us of control, misuse of authority, or moments when leadership failed us.

But biblical submission was never meant to silence leaders it was meant to protect the mission.

After World War II, General Douglas MacArthur met with a Japanese general to receive his formal surrender. The Japanese general extended his hand to shake, but MacArthur refused, saying, "I cannot shake your hand until you first surrender your sword."[22]

This story illustrates a truth about submission: many of us want to "shake hands" with God while still holding onto the sword of our will. Until we surrender our will, we cannot truly walk in unity with Him—or those He has placed over us.

Submission is not just a command; it is a pathway to spiritual growth, protection, and fruitfulness in leadership. For all of us, submission to God and to the authority He sets up is not optional. It is essential to become the kind of leader who inspires others to follow Christ.

Submission is not blind obedience or loss of identity it is the decision to trust God's order more than our own preferences

A GENERATION WRESTLING WITH AUTHORITY

In today's culture, the word "submission" is often viewed as a negative term. As John Piper puts it: "Anything that enhances my individual liberty to do as I please is good, and anything that encumbers me is bad. That is the spirit we breathe in America."

This mindset has infiltrated the minds of our young people, creating resistance to authority and undermining the blessings of submission. Yet the Bible teaches that submission is a gift—not a restriction. It protects us, shapes us, and aligns us with God's mission.

Today's youth often find themselves at odds with traditional authority figures. This tension is not merely anecdotal but is supported by research and observations:

Young people often feel a sense of equality. What I mean is middle and high school-aged members of Generation Z often view themselves as equals to adults, including parents and teachers. This perspective leads them to feel comfortable asserting their opinions, sometimes challenging traditional hierarchies. Think of the "know-it-all" stereotype where someone, no matter if they have zero ability in an area, will act as if they are the leading voice on a topic. This younger generation has become "know-it-alls" on performance enhancers due to their advance access to information through cell phones.

If you are a teacher or professor, you may have met or seen this in your students today. There is a strong resistance in educational settings. Educators have noted an increase in students openly challenging authority, with remarks like, "You can't talk to me like that; I'll disrespect you if you disrespect me," becoming more common. Now their home life plays a significant role in the lack of respect for authority, but again, due to social media and the trends that stem from watching people disrespect others for humor, it also plays a factor.

There is the impact of law enforcement interactions: Youth who experience police stops report higher levels of psychological distress, which can lead to disengagement from school activities. This cycle underscores the complex relationship between authority and youth behavior.

Recognizing this dynamic is crucial for parents, educators, and leaders. We must have a desire for autonomy. Adolescents' challenges to authority often stem from a natural developmental drive toward independence. Understanding this can help adults respond with empathy rather than confrontation.

Not only is a desire for autonomy, but also modeling respectful authority, I would argue, is the most critical piece in solving the disrespectful nature we see in young people today. By showing consistent, respectful authority, adults can help youth understand the balance between autonomy and submission.

A note for parents. It all starts at home. Look at what the Apostle instructs us in Ephesians 6:1-4 ESV Children, obey your parents in the Lord, for this is right. 2 "Honor your father and mother" (this is the first commandment with a promise), 3 "that it may go well with you and that you may live long in the land." 4 Fathers, do not provoke your children to anger, but bring them up in the discipline and instruction of the Lord.

What they see is what they will be. Your example is the best sermon your kids will ever hear and the only one they will remember the most. Children learn obedience, respect, and submission as they see their parents submitting to and obeying God. Parents are under God's authority both in their roles to one another and in their roles as parents. Children are watching how we obey God. Let us teach them well!

> **"What they see is what they will be. Your example is the best sermon your kids will ever hear and the only one they will remember the most."**

THE PROBLEM WITH PRIDE

Why would most of us reject or be opposed to submission? It is because we fall into a mindset driven by pride:

- "That person can't tell me anything."

- "I don't agree with that decision so that I won't follow it."

- "Why can't we do things my way?"

This attitude not only hinders our personal growth but also breeds division, gossip, and obstacles within the body of Christ. Division and gossip are two examples of pride and self exaltation, because they place us in the driver's seat and other people beneath us through our rude and demeaning conduct. This pride can cause a separation in a marriage, or Pastors to be territorial when it comes to having a church in the same city. Pride, as we know, was the catalyst for Satan to lose his status as an angel. We cannot underestimate the power pride has to ruin our lives and the ripple effect it can cause to the people closest to us.

Paul warns us in Romans 16:17-18 ESV 17 I appeal to you, brothers, to watch out for those who cause divisions and create obstacles contrary to the doctrine that you have been taught; avoid them. 18 For such persons do not serve our Lord Christ, but their own appetites, and by smooth talk and flattery they deceive the hearts of the naive.

In other words, Paul advises against associating with people who have a big appetite. He is not talking about when you are starving, and you begin to crave a fresh bowl of Chipotle with steak, white rice, black beans, the trinity of salsas, light sour cream, and a plethora of cheese with a tortilla on the side. Is that my order at Chipotle? Yes, is it delicious? Yes, but this is not the point! Paul is warning us to be aware of people's appetite for division and gossip, so we avoid them. Think for a second about a place where a high volume of gossip takes place and with whom. If you guessed teenagers on social media or at school, you are correct.

We must teach teenagers the art of discernment, to avoid becoming enticed by the allure of gossip, and to be people who submit to the Word of God. As they submit and obey the Word of God, we will begin to witness a generation that ends the rise of bullying and online harassment as they let the Word of God mold and shape them. If they see their parents and leaders practicing humility, not just at church but in the unseen places closed to the public eye. If we can emulate Jesus and follow His example of submission, we can witness revival in the hearts of our young people.

SUBMISSION IN ACTION: JESUS AS OUR EXAMPLE

Notice how all of Jesus' earthly ministry flowed from His submission to the Father. The language of submission Jesus would use was this:

- "I only do what the Father tells me to do."

- "I only go where the Father tells me to go."

- "I only say what the Father wants me to say."

Even in His most difficult moment, in the Garden of Gethsemane, Jesus prayed, "Not as I will, but as You will" (Matthew 26:39). Yes, Jesus eventually surrendered to commit to His fathers will but look at what he says earlier in verse 39 Going a little farther, he fell with his face to the ground and prayed, "My Father, if it is possible, may this cup be taken from me…" It can almost seem like Jesus is pleading to His father asking Him, "Is there another way?" "Do we have to do it this way?"

A key point we see here is that Submission is not submission until it is tested by disagreement.

It is easy to follow when we agree, but real submission is revealed in conflict. What are we showing to young people when we have disagreements with leadership decisions? Parents, when you and your spouse are in the middle of tension, what are your children seeing? What happens in my heart when I don't get what I want?"

"A key point we see here is that Submission is not submission until it is tested by disagreement."

Everyone will find themselves in the arena of disagreement. Let us be honest, turning the other cheek or being the bigger person is not always as easy as we would hope. Still, it is in these moments that the power of submission can reveal its true colors and serve as a teaching point for young people when they enter that arena and have a Godly example to lean on.

If submission was essential for Jesus, how much more is it necessary for us as leaders? Here's why submission is the key to success in ministry:

It Keeps Us Aligned with God's Mission. Submission to spiritual authority helps us stay focused on the mission: bringing people to Jesus. It ensures we are not distracted by personal agendas or pride.

Healthy authority does not diminish calling — it develops it.

It Protects Us from Ourselves. Just as NFL legend Tom Brady submitted to a trainer to stay at the top of his game, spiritual submission keeps us accountable and prevents us from falling into blind spots.

It Teaches Us Humility. Obedience does not always require agreement. When we choose to submit even when we disagree, we cultivate humility and trust in God's plan. And remember this – you can only exercise as much authority as you are submitted to.

BIBLICAL SUBMISSION IN THE CHURCH

The writer of Hebrews outlines three responsibilities every Christian has toward spiritual leaders:

First, we are to **Remember Them** (Hebrews 13:7-9). We are called to recognize and follow leaders who are faithful to God's Word and show godly character. While leaders may come and go, Jesus stays constant, as Warren Wiersbe said, "Never build your life on any servant of God. Build your life on Jesus Christ. He never changes."

Next, we are to **Obey Them** (Hebrews 13:17). Submission does not mean blind obedience to unqualified leaders; instead, it involves recognizing the authority of godly leaders and cooperating with them for the good of the Church. As a next-generation pastor at my church, I am under the authority of our Lead Pastor. I choose to obey him, regardless of whether I agree with his decisions. I understand that God has placed him over me as the spiritual authority in our Church.

What makes it easier for me to submit to his authority is my belief that this aligns with the will of God, as backed by Scripture, and my recognition of my lead pastor as an example of someone worth following. As 1 Peter 5:3 reminds us, pastors and leaders are called to lead by example, not through dictatorship. My pastor continually works to foster a culture in our church that emphasizes collaboration over competition. He carries out this by leading from the front.

Lastly, we are to **Greet Them** (Hebrews 13:24). Paul's example of greeting church leaders with grace and peace teaches us the importance of keeping healthy and respectful relationships with our leaders.

BREAKING DOWN BARRIERS TO SUBMISSION

I understand that ministry is not always easy. People can hurt us, and it is often said that the best part of ministry is the people, while the worst part is also the people. The hurt you have experienced or are currently dealing with may lead you to resist submission. However, do not let past experiences become a barrier to a blessing.

Learn to overcome these barriers by recognizing the enemy's tactics. Satan wants us to perceive submission as weak or unimportant, knowing that such perceptions lead to division and disunity. Therefore, we must be on guard against bitterness. Hebrews 12:15 warns us against allowing a "root of bitterness" to grow in our hearts, as it poisons relationships and hinders spiritual growth.

While we submit to human authority, we must focus on Jesus as our supreme authority. When we fully submit to Jesus, submission to human authority

> **"While we submit to human authority, we must focus on Jesus as our supreme authority. When we fully submit to Jesus, submission to human authority becomes easier."**

becomes easier. Obedience to God's commands brings blessings, as promised in Deuteronomy 28:1-6:

"If you fully obey the Lord your God and carefully follow all His commands I give you today, the Lord your God will set you high above all the nations on earth. All these blessings will come on you and accompany you if you obey the Lord your God: You will be blessed in the city and blessed in the country. The fruit of your womb will be blessed, and the crops of your land and the young of your livestock—the calves of your herds and the lambs of your flocks. Your basket and your kneading trough will be blessed. You will be blessed when you come in and blessed when you go out."

LEADING THE NEXT GENERATION THROUGH SUBMISSION

As we have discussed a lot already in this part of the book Gen Z and Alpha are watching how we lead. They value authenticity and respect but often struggle with authority. By modeling submission, we teach them how to: Follow God's Design for Leadership: Submission is not about power—it is about trust and alignment with God's mission. Work as a Team: Leaders who submit to one another create unity, showing students the beauty of serving together for a common purpose. Trust God's Sovereignty: When we submit to imperfect leaders, we show faith in God's ability to work through them.

The story of General MacArthur reminds us that surrender is the first step to partnership. When we lay down the "sword" of our will and submit to God and His authority, we unlock the blessings of unity, protection, and purpose.

As leaders, submission is not just for our benefit—it is for the benefit of those we serve. When we lead with humility and obedience, we create a culture that reflects Christ and inspires the next generation to follow Him wholeheartedly.

Leaders who understand submission do not lead with insecurity they lead with confidence. They know who they are, where they are planted, and who they are accountable to. And when leaders submit themselves to God's design for authority, the mission does not suffer it thrives. Because submission, when done God's way, always creates space for growth, trust, and lasting impact.

Let us choose submission, knowing it is not a restriction but a doorway to God's best for our lives and ministries.

REFLECTION QUESTIONS

Where do I struggle most to submit to spiritual authority?

Do I truly believe that authority is God's idea for my protection?

What happens in my heart when I don't get my way?

How has rebellion – even subtle rebellion- shown up in my life?

————————

Chapter 4

Character That Is Consistent

22 throw off your old sinful nature and your former way of life, which is corrupted by lust and deception.23 Instead, let the Spirit renew your thoughts and attitudes. 24 Put on your new nature, created to be like God—truly righteous and holy. Ephesians 4:22-24

Big idea: Consistency is the proof of character – who you are every day matters more than who you are on your best day.

WHAT DEFINES SUCCESS?

One of the greatest tensions leaders face is the gap between who we are in public and who we are in private.

It is possible to lead faithfully on a stage while quietly drifting off it. And over time, inconsistency does not just weaken our leadership — it erodes trust.

Pete Rose once said, "Creating success is tough. But keeping it is tougher. You have to keep producing; you can't ever stop."[23] In ministry, the same principle applies. It is one thing to experience moments of success, but supporting that success requires more than talent, vision, or challenging work. It requires a consistent character—a life that honors God in both private and public, day after day.

The world celebrates charisma, but God blesses character. If our character consistently honors God, He will bless our success continually. But this kind of character does not just happen; it is built intentionally, one decision at a time.

This chapter is about cultivating the kind of character that reflects Christ not just in public moments but in the quiet, unseen spaces where true integrity is formed. If we are going to teach the next generation about Godly character, learning how to model it is necessary.

4 QUALITIES OF HIGH CHARACTER

1. Character is Shown in Public but Sown in Private.

"For all that is secret will eventually be brought into the open, and everything that is concealed will be brought to light and made known to all."—Luke 8:17 (NLT)

Your public life will always reflect your private habits. My father always used to tell me this phrase when I was training to play collegiate football. Whenever I started to feel complacent with my success in the weight room or on the field, he would remind me, "Champions are made when no one is looking." What he meant was that anyone can excel when the coach's attention is on them. There is that extra motivation

"Your public life will always reflect your private habits."

that the need for approval will naturally drive us to push ourselves, but what about when no one is around to watch, such as when your pastor is not watching you or your principal is not watching you? Who we are when no one is looking, and who we are when everyone is watching.

I have heard it said that the real you is who you are in secret.

So, ask yourself today:

- How do I act when no one is watching?

- What thoughts, habits, and decisions dominate my private moments?

Our personal devotion decides the direction of our ministry. If we neglect our time with God, our public ministry will lack power and depth. As leaders, we must assume that what we do in private will eventually be made public.

Let me challenge you with this question. If what you are about to do were made public, would you still do it? Would you still watch it? Would you still say it?

Character is not formed in moments of visibility — it is formed in patterns of obedience no one applauds.

2. Character Triumphs Over Talent.

Proverbs tells us, "Better is a poor man who walks in his integrity than a rich man who is crooked in his ways." Proverbs 28:6 (ESV)

The truth is, Talent may open doors, but only character keeps them open. In a world that idolizes skill and performance, God values integrity above all else. In ministry, it is easy to focus on results, such as attendance numbers, social media metrics, or sermon reviews. But these markers of success are temporary. True success comes from being good, not just doing good.

There is a story about Legendary UCLA basketball coach John Wooden, who won 10 NCAA Championships and is considered the greatest college basketball coach of all time. He built a dynasty by emphasizing character over talent. At the start of every season, he taught his players how to put on their socks correctly—a lesson in humility and attention to detail. Wooden believed, "Winning takes talent; to repeat it takes character."[24]

The moral of the story is that collective character in a team leads to lasting success. It is not about how well we perform individually but how faithfully we work together. What would your ministry look like if you had a culture where all your youth leaders focused on doing the little things right? Showing up on time, looking for the student on the front patio of your church who is alone and talking to them, leading in worship by lifting their hands and showing their passion in front of the students to teach them how to worship. The reality is, especially in student ministry, we focus on the big over the little, and it is hurting our young people because they will always catch a stray from our ego. When we think our talent on the platform or following on social media is what leads to success. They play a part, but not the central part.

Remember why you got into youth ministry in the first place, remember why you wanted to enter the education world, and remember why you prayed for children. Do not let your talent turn into ego, and do not let your ego destroy the call of God over your life.

> **"Do not let your talent turn into ego, and do not let your ego destroy the call of God over your life."**

3. Character Is Rooted in Humility.

James says, "Humble yourselves before the Lord, and He will lift you up." James 4:10. True character begins with humility—never being too big to do the insignificant things. It is about prioritizing service over recognition, people over pride.

Humility is what keeps us grounded in God's truth, even when we are tempted by ego or applause. It reminds us that every victory, every opportunity, and every blessing is from Him. What small tasks or overlooked opportunities is God calling you to embrace with humility?

4. Character Is Diligent in the Details.

"If it is to lead, do it diligently."—Romans 12:8 (NIV)

The Greek word for diligence, *spoude,* implies an eye for excellence and a deep sense of care in everything we do. For Christians, diligence means doing all things as an act of worship, with both love and excellence.

Examples of Diligence in Leadership:

- Preparing for a meeting as if it were a sermon.

- Following up with a student who shared their struggles.

- Practicing what you preach—literally.

Martin Luther said it best: "The Christian shoemaker does his duty not by putting little crosses on the shoes, but by making good shoes, because God is interested in good craftsmanship." [25] Diligence transforms ordinary tasks into extraordinary acts of worship. It takes consistent character in action. Living with consistent character is not about perfection; it is about daily faithfulness. It is choosing integrity when no one is watching, humility when recognition is not guaranteed, and diligence when the work feels mundane.

Proverbs 22:1 reminds us: "A good name is to be chosen rather than great riches, and favor is better than silver or gold." For youth pastors and leaders, this is a call to live in such a way that the next generation sees the character of Christ reflected in us.

THE EXAMPLE WE SET FOR THE NEXT GENERATION

As we have discussed already, Gen Z and Alpha are seeking leaders who are genuine, consistent, and Christ-like. They have grown up in a world filled with scandals, broken promises, and fleeting fame. What they need are leaders whose public and private lives match.

Here's how consistent character affects the next generation:

1. **It Builds Trust:** Students are more likely to follow leaders they can rely on to act with integrity.

2. **It Models Jesus:** Consistent character shows them what it looks like to live out the Gospel daily.

3. **It Inspires Faithfulness:** When students see leaders being faithful in the little things, they are encouraged to do the same.

BECOMING LEADERS' WORTH FOLLOWING

Consistent character is not a "one and done" achievement—it is a daily choice to reflect Christ in all we do. It is about sowing integrity in private so we can reap trust and influence in public.

When we live with a character that honors God, we set a foundation not only for our own ministry success but for the spiritual growth of the next generation.

So, ask yourself: What kind of character are you cultivating today? What do people see when they see you—not just on the stage, but in the everyday details of your life?

God honors leaders who honor Him, both in public and in private. Let us commit to being those leaders, for His glory and the good of those we serve.

Consistent character does not happen overnight, but it always leaves a legacy. Leaders who live the same life in every room build trust that can carry weight over time. If we want to lead the next generation well, our faith must be more than visible it must be reliable. Because when character is consistent, leadership becomes credible.

REFLECTION QUESTIONS

Where does inconsistency show up in my life or habits?

What private areas need to catch up with my public leadership?

What excuses do I make that keep me from being faithful?

What patterns from my past still influence how I show up?

———————

Chapter 5

Worship That Works

"Whatever you do, work at it with all your heart, as working for the Lord, not for human masters." Colossians 3:23

Big idea: Worship is not just what we sing – it is the work we offer God with our whole lives.

THE MYTH OF THE DIVIDE

Worship is often measured by how it makes us feel. But biblical worship has always been measured by how it forms us.

Worship that works is not louder, longer, or more emotional it is obedient, faithful, and consistent, even when no one is watching.

Let me ask you this. What comes to mind when you hear the word "spiritual"? Most people might think of prayer, fasting, worship, and reading scripture, which are certainly valid associations. However, let me ask you another question: What about hard work or consistency?

There is a subtle misconception that often creeps into ministry: the idea that the spiritual and the practical exist in separate realms. You know what I mean—prayer feels sacred, but spreadsheets? Not so much. Preaching seems holy, while setting up chairs or following up with a student who has disappeared from your radar feels just like part of the job, right?

This misconception is dangerous. When we separate the sacred from the practical, we create a version of Christianity that thrives on Sundays but collapses during the rest of the week.

Unbeknownst to us, the next generation is watching how we live. Remember the moment you stepped into leadership? Or when your family and friends discovered you are a Christian? All eyes turn to you.

While this may feel like a lot of pressure, the truth is that we want those eyes on us so we can point people to Jesus. How we live—not just within the church but outside it—will significantly impact the people we seek to reach.

What they need to see is rare yet straightforward: that everything we do can be an act of worship—especially the things no one applauds. My hope with this chapter is to teach us that there is no separation between what feels "spiritual" and what feels "practical" in the kingdom of God. The Bible makes it clear: prayer gives us vision; worship provides perspective. However, hard work gives those things legs. We must understand that hard work is deeply spiritual.

> **"When we separate the sacred from the practical, we create a version of Christianity that thrives on Sundays but collapses during the rest of the week."**

In ministry, it is possible to have passion but lack perseverance – passion without perseverance burns out. This is why we often undervalue the "non-spiritual" tasks:

- Showing up on time

- Being excellent in planning

- Being reliable in the tiny things

- Following through on responsibilities

We can assume that these activities are merely administrative tasks or planning efforts. However, when done with the right heart, they become acts of worship. These actions are profoundly spiritual and contribute to building trust, credibility, and character—qualities that God uses to multiply ministry and shape our lives. Hard work and commitment in ministry are no less spiritual; they are expressions of how we live out our worship. You do not need a platform to be spiritual; you need faithfulness. God not only anoints your prayer time; He also anoints your planning time, your setup time, and your follow-through.

We often focus on just a few aspects of our lives, neglecting the fact that all parts of our lives are spiritual in nature. When we lose sight of this, those aspects lose their value, and what loses value often gets overlooked. This is like the storyline in Toy Story: as Andy grew older, his toys lost their significance and were eventually forgotten.

THE WORSHIP IN WORK

Romans 12:1 sets the tone: "Therefore, I urge you, brothers and sisters, in view of God's mercy, to offer your bodies as a living sacrifice, holy and pleasing to God—this is your true and proper worship."

Paul does not say, "Lift your hands more." He says, offer your life. Your actual, daily life—your thoughts, your actions, your habits, your Monday mornings. That is the kind of worship God desires.

So, when you stay late to clean up after youth group, type out a devotional with no response, pour into a student who is drifting, edit slides, make coffee, and set up chairs… that is worship.

It may not feel like it. It may not look like it. But if it is done for Jesus, it is worship.

THE THEOLOGY OF SWEAT

Let us talk theology—real theology. Because for too long, we have made hard work seem like a second-class spiritual practice. But Scripture says otherwise.

Colossians 3:23 reminds us: "Whatever you do, work at it with all your heart, as working for the Lord, not for human masters."

It does not say, "When you're leading worship" or "When you're preaching." It says whatever you do. That includes organizing games, replying to emails, prepping lessons, and resetting chairs for the fiftieth time. When done unto the Lord, it is not just administration—it is adoration.

Break this verse down:

"Whatever you do" – not just leading, but scheduling, setting up, and text follow-ups.

"Work willingly" – not halfway. Not when it feels good. Willingly.

"For the Lord" – Everything we do becomes sacred when the audience is Jesus.

"You will receive a reward" – The world may not see, but God always sees.

"God has no favorites" – He honors both the worship leader and the one plugging in the mic. And that's why hard work matters – even when it is unseen or uncelebrated

Tim Keller puts it this way: "Everyone will be forgotten, nothing we do will make any difference, and all good endeavors, even the best, will come to naught… unless there is God. If the God of the Bible exists, and there is a true reality beneath and behind this one… then every good endeavor, even the simplest one, pursued in response to God's calling, can matter forever."[26]

Your preparation, your consistency, your faithfulness—they echo in eternity when done for Christ.

This is where many leaders burn out or get bitter. They start to believe the lie that only "anointed" things are worth doing. But listen, if Jesus could spend most of His earthly life swinging a hammer as a carpenter, don't you think He sees our behind-the-scenes labor as sacred too?

"No crooked table-legs or ill-fitting drawers ever, I dare swear, came out of the carpenter's shop at Nazareth. Nor, if they did, could anyone believe that they were made by the same hand that made heaven and earth." [27]

This quote, from Dorothy Sayers' essay "Why Work?", highlights the spiritual nature of work by linking it to Jesus' own ethic—implying that his carpentry in Nazareth produced only quality goods, reflecting divine craftsmanship. If Jesus worked hard, what gives us the right to be lazy in ministry? Jesus is our most significant example, but we also see this through Paul, who emphasizes the importance of it.

PAUL'S WORK ETHIC

Paul did not just write about grace—he worked hard. Like, hard. In all the Scriptures, no one talks about work more than the apostle Paul. Paul himself was a tentmaker. Such work was an especially pressing issue in Thessalonica, where some in the church were lazy, refusing to work — waiting, they said, for Christ's imminent return. Paul saw it as a spiritual sounding covering for laziness. He put himself and Timothy forward as examples of hard work.

"Don't you remember… how hard we worked among you? Night and day we toiled to earn a living so that we would not be a burden… as we preached God's Good News."—1 Thessalonians 2:9 (NLT)

Paul is preaching, yes – but he is also working. Why? Because the Gospel deserves our best effort.

"We were not idle… We worked hard day and night…"—1 Thessalonians 3:7–8

Paul knew the transforming power of the Spirit and expected moochers and thieves alike to find a new work ethic once they came to Christ. Paul was saying: I did not just preach with my mouth—I preached with my schedule. I did not just bring the Word—I brought my full self to the mission.

Ephesians 4:28 NLT 28 If you are a thief, quit stealing. Instead, use your hands for good hard work, and then give generously to others in need.

People who do not work hard are a burden and can hinder the spread of the gospel. Paul is not just modeling ministry – he is modeling maturity. That is leadership. That is character. That is what Gen Z and Alpha need to see. Because they are not impressed with titles, they are inspired by authenticity.

PROVERBS, NEHEMIAH, AND THE LAZY FIELD

Let us not forget the warning from Proverbs 24: "I walked by the field of a lazy person… it was overgrown with thorns. Its walls were broken down… A little extra sleep… and poverty will pounce like a thief."—Proverbs 24:30–34

The writer names 3 emotional triggers that keep us from working:

1- Sleep – avoiding responsibility

2- Slumber – afraid to start

3- Folding of hands – giving in to apathy

Sleep is motivated by the desire to avoid the stress and pressure of responsibility. Slumber is being afraid to start because we do not think we will be able to finish. The folding of the hands to rest is the inevitable apathy that occurs when sleep and slumber have evolved from temporary emotions to become a persistent, habitual response to life. The best way to overcome avoidance, fear, and apathy is to understand that they are driven by emotions – many of which are irrational – and then choose to pray.

That field did not fall apart overnight. It was a little decision. A few skipped follow-ups. A few unchecked habits. A few "I'll do it next week" moments. And soon the field—the ministry, the relationship, the soul—is a mess.

The opposite is Nehemiah: "They were trying to intimidate us… But I prayed, 'Now strengthen my hands.'"—Nehemiah 6:9

What did Nehemiah do when he was tired and overwhelmed? He did not quit. He did not push harder in his own strength. He prayed for God to strengthen his hands – and he kept working. Nehemiah saw the dream God laid on his heart come true, because he relied on prayer to make his hands strong enough to keep working. Whatever takes the wind out of our sails and prevents us from working towards our dream, it is at those moments that we must return to God, just like Nehemiah, and ask Him to strengthen our hands until what we imagined by faith becomes a reality.

That is a prayer every leader needs. "God, I am tired. I feel stretched. But strengthen my hands."

That is worship.

WHEN NO ONE SEES YOU

Let us be honest: sometimes you serve and wonder if it even matters. You plan the event, text the kids, prepare the message… and three students show up. You pour into a teen for months… and they still make a mess of their life.

You want to say, "Is this even working?" Here is the thing—God never asked us to measure our worship by results. He just asked us to give Him our best.

The unseen work is often the most anointed. Heaven is watching, even when the room is half-full. Faithfulness is fruitfulness.

So how does this play out? Here is a picture of worship that works: Monday: You block off time to plan next week's youth night. It is slow, you feel uninspired, but you are doing it as unto Jesus. Tuesday: You show up early to help a student prep for a college interview. They seem distracted, but you stay present. Wednesday: You teach your Bible lesson and wonder if anyone even listened. You plant seeds anyway. Thursday: You rest. You honor the Sabbath. You trust that your ministry does not rise and fall on your hustle. Friday: Follow up with the new student who visited last week. They do not text back. You do it anyway. Saturday: You lead a volunteer meeting and celebrate small wins. Sunday: You worship—fully. Not just on the platform, but in how you welcome others, encourage someone, or pick up trash off the floor.

All of it is worship. All of it matters.

> **"The unseen work is often the most anointed. Heaven is watching, even when the room is half-full. Faithfulness is fruitfulness."**

Discipline is not legalism — its devotion expressed over time.

This is not just true for youth pastors; it applies to all pastors. Remember, Parents and teachers—you are in ministry too.

When you: Pack a lunch with a note inside. Pray with your kids before school. Grade papers late at night. Show up early for a parent-teacher conference.

That is worship. You are discipling by your diligence. The next generation is not just shaped by what we say—they are shaped by what we model.

Here is what we know about these generations: They crave authenticity. They are skeptical of performance. They are hungry for purpose.

They do not want hype. They want honesty. And when they see a leader who sweeps floors, stays after, follows through, and owns their mistakes? That is who they respect.

They are looking for someone to become, not just someone to listen to. Your hard work may not trend. But it may be the very thing that shows a student what faithfulness looks like.

THE ALTAR IS EVERYWHERE

What if we stopped separating the sacred from the scheduled? What if your calendar, team meetings, and late-night prep were seen as altars of worship? We pray as it depends on God, but we work as it depends on us!

Here is a Challenge: Commit to one area you will treat more seriously as worship: prep, follow through, presence, or excellence. Circle it. Own it. Commit to it. Because this is more than work – it is worship that works.

Martin Luther King Jr from his speech "The Three Dimensions of a Complete Life" "What I'm saying to you this morning, my friends, even if it falls your lot to be a street sweeper, go on out and sweep streets like Michelangelo painted pictures; sweep streets like Handel and Beethoven composed music; sweep streets like Shakespeare wrote poetry; sweep streets so well that all the host of heaven and earth will have to pause and say, "Here lived a great street sweeper who swept his job well."

"If you can't be a pine on the top of a hill, be a scrub in the valley—but be the best little scrub on the side of the hill, be a bush if you can't be a tree. If you can't be a highway, just be a trail. If you can't be the sun be a star; It isn't by size that you win or fail—Be the best of whatever you are. And when you do this, when you do this, you've mastered the length of life."[28]

Replace "street sweeper" with "youth pastor," "teacher," or "parent." That is us. We do the work no one sees, and we do it for an audience of One.

Let us be leaders who live Romans 12:1. Let us be the ones who prepare the room, send the text, clean the mess, hold the line, and walk with students even when they walk slowly. Let us be the ones who make ministry more than a moment. Because when our hearts are surrendered, and our hands are faithful, that is worship that works.

Worship that works does not always move a crowd, but it always moves the heart of God. It is found in obedience, in showing up, and in choosing faithfulness long after the music fades. If we want to lead the next generation well, our worship must be more than expressive it must be enduring.

REFLECTION QUESTIONS

Where in your ministry or family life have you started to see certain tasks as "less spiritual"?

What would change if you approached your schedule like a living sacrifice?

Where have you become weary in doing good?

How can you pray like Nehemiah: "Strengthen my hands"? What is one ordinary task this week you can treat like worship?

Chapter 6

The Rhythms of Rest

"Take my yoke upon you and learn from me, for I am gentle and humble in heart, and you will find rest for your souls. For my yoke is easy, and my burden is light." Matthew 11:29-30

Big Idea: Rest is not a reward- it is a requirement for leaders who want to finish well.

SHARPEN THE AXE

A man once challenged another to an all-day wood-chopping contest. The challenger worked tirelessly, stopping only for a quick lunch. The other man, however, took frequent breaks. At the end of the day, the challenger was shocked to find the other man had chopped significantly more wood. "How did you do it?" the challenger asked. "You rested more than I did!" The other man replied, "What you didn't notice was that during my breaks, I was sharpening my axe." The lesson is simple: Rest makes you sharper.[29]

In ministry, rest is not a luxury—it is a necessity. Without it, we risk burnout, poor decision-making, and losing the joy that drew us into serving in the first place.

Burnout rarely announces itself. It creeps in quietly disguised as faithfulness, sacrifice, and commitment.

Many leaders do not ignore rest because they do not believe in it. They ignore it because they believe the mission cannot survive without them. But when rest is neglected, the cost is never just personal it eventually spills into our leadership, our families, and our faith.

WHY THIS MATTERS FOR CHARACTER AND CALLING

Before we can talk about creating community or shaping culture, we must ask ourselves: What kind of leaders are we becoming? Reaching the next generation is not just about strategy—it is about sustainability. Because if we are going to model the character of Christ to students, we must learn to live like Christ ourselves. And Jesus was not rushed, reactive, or burned out. He was rooted. Rhythmic. Rested. Students do not just need leaders with charisma. They need leaders with sustainability—leaders who live what they preach and stay spiritually healthy over time. That kind of depth does not come from hustle; it comes from rhythm. If we want to raise the next generation to follow Jesus with joy and endurance, then we need to lead from a rested and rooted place.

In this chapter, we explore why rest is not a sign of weakness, but rather wisdom—and how embracing the pace of Jesus is one of the most powerful things we can do to lead well in the long haul.

THE REST JESUS OFFERS

Jesus promises rest for our souls, yet so many of us feel anything but rested. Instead, we are tired, stressed, and overwhelmed by the demands of ministry. We read His words in Matthew 11 and wonder: "Jesus, are you sure?" "Is this rest only for heaven, not here and now?"

The truth is that the rest Jesus offers is not found in escape but in alignment. It is not about doing less; it is about doing life His way. As Adam Mabry puts it: "The art of rest is about learning how to rest with Jesus, not from Jesus."[30]

One of the questions often asked by young leaders is, "How do you combat burnout?" or "What steps should I take when experiencing burnout?" The term "burnout" refers to the state in which an individual feels exhausted or overwhelmed due to prolonged or intense involvement in ministry activities. We can all feel burnout. Whether you are a coach. A youth leader or teacher dealing with young people asks a lot from us. I worry that the solution many use to alleviate burnout is to stop serving or disconnect from ministry for a period.

Taking a break in a relationship often proves ineffective, as one cannot take a break from being a disciple. There is no "off" switch for discipleship. Stepping away from serving the church does not address burnout; rather, it can be a catalyst for unbelief.

What do I mean? During my time in youth ministry, several individuals would meet with me to discuss their feelings of exhaustion or the need for a break to recharge. In many cases, the issue was not fatigue but hidden sin or undisclosed agendas at play. They used burnout as a justification to step away, which always seemed right at the time.

I understand that people can be tired due to stress from work, school, or home life. However, if Jesus is our source of rest, disconnecting from that source will not help us; instead, it will harm us. Rest is not a reward for finishing the work it is an act of trust that God is still working when we stop.

"Rest is not a reward for finishing the work it is an act of trust that God is still working when we stop."

Leaders who refuse to rest do not become more productive they become more brittle. Over time, exhaustion dulls discernment, shortens patience, and weakens compassion. What begins as overcommitment eventually becomes misalignment. And by the time many leaders realize they need rest, the damage has already started.

UNDERSTANDING THE YOKE

Jesus uses the image of a yoke—a wooden crosspiece that binds two animals together, allowing them to share a burden. When training a young ox, farmers would yoke it to an older, stronger ox. The experienced ox bore most of the burden and guided the younger one.

This is the invitation Jesus extends to us: to be yoked with Him, to walk at His pace, and to let Him carry the heaviest part of the load. But too often, we resist the yoke. We try to do ministry in our own strength, and in doing so, we miss out on the rest and peace He offers. Pete Marshall says it like this, "In the name of Jesus Christ, who was never in a hurry, we pray, O God, that You will slow us down, for we know that we live too fast." If you want to experience the full life of Jesus, you must adopt the lifestyle of Jesus.

Many of us struggle to rest because of the systems we have created in our lives. As John Mark Comer writes: "Every system is perfectly designed to get the results it gets."[31] If our lives are producing anxiety, burnout, and stress, it is a sign that something in our system is off. Ministry is demanding, but God never intended for us to carry it alone. Here is the problem: You will never experience proper rest if you live as two different people—one in ministry and another in private.

There is tranquility to be found when we are the same people on the platform as we are off it, not hiding our flaws but allowing our vulnerabilities to minister to the people we lead or the children we parent. I am not advocating that everyone in your youth group or life needs to know all your sins. The point I am trying to make is that rest can be found by not having to always "be on."

In my life, this is not easy. As a pastor, the expectation is often that because I preach on prayer with authority, it must mean I am great at prayer. I am not particularly strong in my prayer life, and there is a significant need for me to improve in this area. Do I know I need to pray more? Yes. Do I feel ashamed to tell you this? No. I am at peace and find rest knowing that I will get better and that Jesus still loves me.

What I will not do is act like I am a prayer warrior 24/7 to everyone I speak with. My pastor side is always on. Do you know why we can be so severely stressed, even though we have a relationship with Jesus? We are not okay with people seeing our scars. Until we can be OK with that, we will never find true rest for our souls.

This is why we must create rhythms of rest. Jesus did not just preach about rest; He modeled it, and so should we. He often withdrew to solitary places to pray and spent time alone with the Father before major decisions and ministry moments.

Here are three keys to cultivating a lifestyle of rest:

1. Rest Takes Commitment

"For all who have entered into God's rest have rested from their labors, just as God did after creating the world. So let us do our best to enter that rest."—Hebrews 4:10-11 (NLT)

Rest is our responsibility. Burnout is not just the result of doing too much; it is often the result of neglecting what matters most. Prioritizing rest requires intentionality and discipline.

> **"Rest is our responsibility. Burnout is not just the result of doing too much; it is often the result of neglecting what matters most."**

For some leaders, rest looks like a true Sabbath. For others, it is creating non-negotiable boundaries around family, sleep, or time with God. The rhythm matters more than the formula but without intentional structure, rest will always be the first thing sacrificed.

Schedule rest like you schedule work. Treat it as non-negotiable time to recharge physically, emotionally, and spiritually.

A word I would like to share with the young leaders at the church is the importance of intentionality. We are intentional about the things we care about. This is just a simple fact. If there is a musical artist whose tour is coming to our city in a few months, we will be intentional about saving money and making sure we are there. If you are a parent with a busy work schedule and your child has a sporting event coming up, you will adjust your calendar to ensure you are there. Why are we not like this with our rest? We pray for it, ask for it, and desire it, yet we are never intentional in making it a possibility. This segways us to our next point.

2. Rest Takes Preparation

Just as athletes prepare rigorously to perform at their best, we must prepare for rest. It is not about doing less but organizing our lives to make rest possible.

Jesus spent 30 years preparing for three years of ministry. Think about that. Many of us can barely wait 30 seconds for hot pockets to be done in the microwave. Jesus took time to make. He did not waste time, and He stayed consistent about his father's business. Even during His ministry, He often withdrew to pray and recharge. His preparation enabled Him to lead from a place of strength.

What habits or routines do you need to adjust to make rest a reality in your life?

3. Rest Takes Trust

Life is hard, and ministry is demanding. But Jesus does not offer escape—He provides equipment. His yoke is not punishment; it is a blessing. We cannot disconnect from Jesus and believe we will connect to the rest we want.

The great evangelist Billy Graham puts it like this, "God knows we need rest, and one of the reasons He established the Sabbath was to give us rest… But God's plan also was to use the Sabbath to turn our hearts and minds toward Him."

An easy life is not an option, but an easy yoke is. When we trust Jesus to set the pace and carry the heaviest burdens, we find rest even amid work.

LIVING THE RESTED LIFE

Rest is not just about taking breaks; it is about aligning your life with Jesus' rhythms. It is about trusting Him with your time, your ministry, and your future.

Dallas Willard says, "Our mistake is to think that following Jesus consists in loving our enemies, going the 'second mile,' and turning the other cheek—while living the rest of our lives just as everyone else around us does. It is a strategy bound to fail."[32]

When Gen Z and Alpha see us constantly overwhelmed or overworked, they begin to assume that's just what faith looks like. But when they see a leader who models rest, margin, and joy—they start to believe that following Jesus might lead to peace. In a world where anxiety and burnout are rising among young people, one of the most countercultural things we can show them is how to live at the pace of grace.

Teenagers today are busier than ever before. My wife works at a private Christian school here in Miami. Sometimes I have the honor of speaking at their chapel or visiting my wife during lunch. During these visits, I connect with and communicate to the students, inviting them to our youth service on Friday nights. Without fail, each student tells me about their schedule and all the things they either must study for (this one I doubt), practice for an upcoming sporting event, rehearsal for the school play, and the list goes on and on. Listening to them share all this can be shocking at times. My heart goes out to them, yes, they are young, and it's an opportune time to do as much as possible, but if we do not teach them to have rhythm of rest, then are we creating leaders who will eventually be crippled by time and work in the future?

DO NOT PLAY INJURED

In many sports films, there is typically a scene depicting an individual who sustains an injury yet continues to strive towards their goal or victory in their respective sport despite the pain. This portrayal aims to inspire the audience to persevere through their own challenges. These scenes are effective but not entirely correct. While many athletes play through injuries, the advice given to athletes when injured in real sports differs from what is portrayed in movies. During my college football career, we were recommended against playing while injured. It may seem unnecessary to emphasize this, as phrases like "tough it out" or "fight through the pain" are commonly expected.

However, there were occasions when the recommendation was made because a player with a severe injury who is not performing at close to 100%, or even 80%, can be considered more of a liability to the team than an asset. It may make for a good story in a film, but in a real-life game, I could be the very reason we lose the game, all because I wanted to tough it out.

Just as a football player who refuses to sit out often ends up becoming a liability on the field, leaders who refuse to rest can hurt the very people they are trying to help. We believe we are being strong by persevering through the exhaustion. Pushing through burnout is just part of the call. However, the truth is that when we lead at 50%, when we are spiritually limping but pretending to be fine, we are not protecting our calling—we are endangering it.

One of the most mature things a leader can do is acknowledge their need for recovery. Rest is not weakness. It is wisdom. And taking time to restore your soul might not look impressive—but it may be the very thing that preserves your leadership for the long haul.

Jesus Practiced Rest—and So Did His Disciples

Jesus consistently withdrew from crowds to be alone with the Father. He rested even when needs were urgent. He paused even when people demanded more. And when His disciples returned from ministry exhausted, Jesus did not push them harder. He invited them away: "Come with me by yourselves to a quiet place and get some rest."

"Rest was not a reward for finishing the mission. It was part of obedience within the mission."

Rest was not a reward for finishing the mission. It was part of obedience within the mission.

If Jesus needed rhythms of withdrawal, so do we.

PRACTICING THE RHYTHMS OF REST

Rest is not accidental. It must be chosen, practiced, and protected.

Daily Rest

Create short moments of stillness with God. Ten minutes of quiet prayer, Scripture, or silence can reset a distracted soul. For students, this may mean replacing scrolling before bed with stillness. For leaders, it means guarding time with God before pouring into others.

Weekly Rest

Practice Sabbath. One day to stop striving. No planning, no emails, no pressure to produce. This is not wasted time—it is refueling time. Leaders model this not only by resting themselves, but by allowing others to lead while they do.

Seasonal Rest

Busy seasons require intentional recovery. Camps, conferences, school semesters, and ministry pushes should be followed by margin. Rest must be scheduled, or it will be sacrificed.

Emotional Rest

God designed us to carry burdens together. Honest conversations, confession, and trusted relationships allow the soul to breathe. Leaders need shepherds too. Students need safe spaces to be known.

Digital Rest

Silence the noise. Fast from constant connectivity. Stillness becomes nearly impossible when life is always loud. Turning down the volume helps us hear God again.

Understand this burnout is not a badge of honor. Rest does not mean you are done—it means you are being sustained. God often does His deepest work in us when we finally slow down. If you do not choose rest, your body eventually will.

The question is not whether you will rest, but whether you will rest by design or by collapse.

STAY SHARP

The rhythms of rest are not a luxury—they are essential for ministry. Just as the woodsman sharpened his axe to work more effectively, we must prioritize rest to serve more faithfully.

God does not call us to exhaustion; He calls us to alignment. By taking on His yoke, we find rest, peace, and the strength to lead well—not just for a season, but for the long haul. John C. Maxwell points out, "True leadership must be for the benefit of the followers, not to enrich the leader."[33]

This young generation needs leadership that is not always exhausted but aggressively fights their fatigue with fierce determination. Something I remind myself of often—and cannot forget because I have it tattooed— is this: "built for the long haul." I want to be intentional, plan, and make time to rest. Whether that means going to bed earlier, running, or planning vacations throughout the year, I do not want to sprint into heaven; I want to limp there because I was able to give it my all. The only way I can do that is by making rest one of my greatest allies.

Rest is not a pause from leadership it is part of it. Leaders who build rhythms of rest are not stepping away from the mission; they are ensuring they can stay in it. If we want to lead the next generation for the long haul, we must learn to trust God enough to stop, knowing He never does.

REFLECTION QUESTIONS

What is one rest rhythm I can commit to this month?

Who can help me maintain healthy boundaries around rest?

How do I know I am running on empty?

When was the last time I truly rested in God's presence?

———

Chapter 7

The Power of Remembering

4 But I have this against you, that you have abandoned the love you had at first. 5 Remember therefore from where you have fallen; repent, and do the works you did at first. If not, I will come to you and remove your lampstand from its place, unless you repent. Revelation 2:4-5

Big Idea: What you remember shapes what you believe—leaders who recognize God's faithfulness can endure any season.

DO NOT FORGET WHERE YOU CAME FROM

Most leaders do not walk away from their calling because they stop believing they walk away because they forget.

They forget what God has already done, what He has already spoken, and why they said yes in the first place. And when memory fades, discouragement grows louder

When you have been walking with Jesus for a while, it is easy to forget where you started. Think back to your earliest days of faith. Maybe it was the altar at a youth camp, or the quiet seat in church where the gospel finally hit home. Perhaps it was that moment you knew God was real because He met you in your darkest place.

The problem is that the longer we lead, the greater the distance grows between us and those first moments. Responsibilities pile up. The grind of ministry wears on us. Before we know it, we are still leading, still serving—but the fire feels dimmer than it used to.

Jesus spoke directly to this in Revelation 2:4-5, when He told the church at Ephesus: "You have forsaken the love you had at first. Consider how far you have fallen! Repent and do the things you did at first."

The Ephesian church was a busy, active, and doctrinally sound community. From the outside, it appeared to be great. But inside, they had lost their "first love."

Leaders, this is a warning for us too. Character is not just about avoiding sin—it is about sustaining passion. It is not enough to perform ministry tasks if our hearts are drifting away from the One for whom we are doing them.

THE TEMPTATION OF DRIFTING

Nobody wakes up one morning and decides, "Today I'll lose my passion for God." Drifting happens slowly. A youth pastor begins to measure their worth by attendance numbers instead of obedience. A parent becomes more focused on managing their kid's behavior than shepherding their heart. A teacher loses sight of their influence in the classroom and slips into autopilot.

It is a slow fade. We do not fall out of love with Jesus overnight—we forget.

Discouragement thrives in forgetfulness. When we lose sight of what God has already done, current challenges begin to feel permanent. But remembering reframes the moment it reminds us that the same God who was faithful then is still faithful now.

This is why remembering is so critical. Remembering is not living in the past—it is using the past as fuel for the future.

"Remembering is not living in the past—it is using the past as fuel for the future."

In the church world, we often view looking back at our past as something to avoid at all costs. The topic of forgetting your past and focusing on your future is commonly used by preachers, as many of us would rather leave our past behind than dwell on it. Consequently, messages like this can resonate strongly with a congregation because they reflect a popular idea.

However, the issue is that sometimes remembering our past can be beneficial in gaining hope for our future.

Throughout Scripture, remembering was never passive — it was practiced.

It is interesting that the Old Testament often tells the people to remember what God has done. The Hebrew verb *zaqan* and it means to remember to do something. The remembering is never just recalling something that happened or something God but remembering what God did to spur us on to faithfulness to us in the past.

Psalm 63:6-7 (AMP) illustrates the Psalmist's reflections on the past: "When I remember you on my bed, I meditate and thoughtfully focus on you in the night watches. For you have been my help, and in the shadow of your wings (where I am always protected), I sing for joy."

Isaiah also emphasizes the power of remembering the past in Isaiah 46:9-10 (NLT), where God tells him, "Remember the things I have done in the past. For I alone am God! I am God, and there is none like me. Only I can tell you the future before it even happens. Everything I plan will come to pass, for I do whatever I wish."

Here is the truth: sometimes we need to return to the basics to move forward. When I reflect on what God has done for His people, including myself, my faith is stirred. If He did it back then, He can do it again!

> **"Here is the truth: sometimes we need to return to the basics to move forward."**

What I have learned from my time in ministry is that keeping passion for something over a prolonged period can be difficult. I love Chipotle. If you have not noticed, this is my 2nd mention of it. I could eat it every day. Yet there are times when, despite my love for it, I do not want to have it and choose something else for lunch.

Longevity is not easy. In America, 50% of marriages end in divorce. When we engage in the same activities for an extended period, the routine can become monotonous and repetitive. This repetitive cycle often leads to temptations to quit, leave, or even cheat in our marriages or ministries.

My concern is that if our passion is not consistent, our purpose may falter. If you are reading this and you have lost your love, feel like quitting, are questioning your calling, or have lost heart, I encourage you to look back and remember why you entered the ministry in the first place. Why did you become a youth leader? A coach? A parent?

BIBLICAL MODELS OF REMEMBERING

The Bible is full of commands to remember. God knew His people were prone to forget, so He built rhythms of remembrance into their lives. Joshua 4: After Israel crossed the Jordan River, God told them to build a pile of stones as a memorial. Why? So future generations would ask, "What do these stones mean?" and parents could retell the story of God's faithfulness.

Passover: Every year, Jewish families retold the story of the Exodus so they would not forget how God delivered them. The Lord's Supper: Jesus said, "Do this in remembrance of me." Communion is built on remembering the cross.

Remembering is not optional—it is essential for sustained faith.

So why do we forget? Why does passion fade? Success dulls urgency. When things are going well, we forget how desperate we were for God in the beginning. Busyness drowns reflection. We run from meeting to meeting, program to program, without time to pause. Pain clouds perspective. Hurt, disappointment, or burnout can cause us to focus more on survival than on gratitude.

For Gen Z and Alpha leaders, this is even more real. The constant noise of social media and cultural pressure makes it easy to live distracted and disconnected. But here is the truth: you cannot lead students into remembering God's faithfulness if you have forgotten it yourself.

PRACTICAL STEPS TO REMEMBER AND REKINDLE

How do we return to our first love? Revelation 2 gives us three steps: "Consider… Repent… Do the things you did at first." Consider this: Take a moment to reflect on where you started. Journal the moments God spoke to you. Revisit the testimonies of students whose lives were changed. Reflection restores perspective. Repent: Acknowledge where you have drifted. Repentance is not just about sin—it is about course correction.

It is saying, "God, I have let the fire fade. Rekindle me again." Do the things you did at first: Go back to the basics. Worship with abandon. Pray like you did when you first believed. Serve with joy. Sometimes the way forward is to return to the simple practices that ignited our passion in the first place.

Consider the church in Ephesus to which this letter is addressed. They were a good church, but something was wrong. Jesus acknowledged all the positive things they were doing—reaching out to others, holding strong services, and keeping healthy small groups—but He still had a complaint against them. The issue was that the Ephesians' church was a "working" church. I think many of us can relate to this. Sometimes, we focus more on working for Jesus rather than simply being with Him.

We can place what we do for Jesus above who we are in Him. The moment we stop being motivated by our love for Jesus, we find ourselves in trouble.

1 Thessalonians 1:3 reminds us: "We remember before our God and Father your work produced by faith, your labor prompted by love, and your endurance inspired by hope in our Lord Jesus Christ."

Let our motivation to serve the next generation be rooted in love—love for our Savior and love for those who are lost.

Think about this: Is it possible to serve, sacrifice, and suffer for Jesus while not truly knowing Him? We need to look deep within ourselves, check our hearts, change our minds, and return to the works we did at first.

I remember a season when I was more focused on building programs than building people. The numbers looked good, but something inside me was empty. Then one night, God reminded me of my own youth group days—stacking chairs, cleaning bathrooms, serving behind the scenes with joy. Back then, I did not care about position. I just wanted to serve Jesus.

That memory wrecked me—in the best way. It pulled me back to a place of gratitude. And from there, passion started to rise again.

Leaders, as I mentioned before, sometimes the way forward is to look back.

Some leaders write prayers down. Others revisit old journals, testimonies, or moments God showed up unmistakably. However, it looks, intentional remembering creates anchors reminders that God has been faithful before and will be faithful again.

This is not just for pastors. Parents—when was the last time you told your kids how God saved you? Teachers—have you shared with students why you chose to teach, and how God called you? Students need to see our passion. They need to hear our stories. If we want them to carry faith, we must remind ourselves where that faith began.

Do not Lose Your First Love

Remembering does not trap us in the past—it fuels our future. Leaders who remember God's faithfulness can persevere through seasons of difficulty without losing their passion. Parents who retell God's goodness create generational faith. Teachers who live with gratitude leave a mark that outlasts the classroom.

So here is the challenge: do not lose your first love. Do not let the ministry become mechanical. Do not let the fire grow cold. Remember. Repent. Repeat the basics.

Because when leaders burn with first love, students will catch the flame.

Remember your impact. It may not feel like it, but you are making an impact on young people. Look back to when you prayed for a student to be saved, and they were. Look back when you baptized a student whom everyone gave up on. Look back at every moment where God showed up and believe Him again.

The Global Youth Culture survey says this, "teens told us that regularly engaging with a community of believers helped them have a more positive outlook on life." [34]

Remember Not to Quit

Everyone remembers the runner who finishes first, but who pays attention to the runner who finishes last? One reporter did at the 1968 Olympic Games in Mexico City. That runner was John Stephen Akhwari of Tanzania. Akhwari fell, injuring his knee and dislocating it. He also smashed his shoulder against the pavement. Most observers, seeing his injuries, assumed he would pull out and go to the hospital. Instead, he received medical attention and returned to the track to continue his race. An hour after the winner, Akhwari crossed the finish line in last place, cheered on by a few thousand spectators who had still been in the stadium after the sun went down. His right leg was bandaged, he was bleeding, and he was clearly in great pain.

As he completed his run, a reporter asked him why he continued despite his injuries. He replied, "My country didn't send me here to start the race. My country sent me here to finish it."[35]

Galatians 6:9 (NLT) states: "So let's not get tired of doing what is good. At just the right time, we will reap a harvest of blessing if we don't give up."

If you do not quit, you win!

Remembering is how leaders stay grounded when seasons change. It keeps us from rewriting God's faithfulness based on temporary circumstances. If we want to lead the next generation with endurance, we must become people who remember not just what God has done, but who He has proven Himself to be.

REFLECTION QUESTIONS

What is one defining moment in your faith journey that you need to revisit and thank God for today?

Where in your life or ministry have you noticed your passion for Jesus starting to fade?

What's one "first love" practice you can return to this week (worship, prayer, serving, testimony)?

How can you model remembrance for the students, children, or peers you influence?

PART 2

COMMUNITY

"The more genuine and the deeper our
community becomes, the more will everything
else between us recede, the more clearly and
purely will Jesus Christ and his work become the
one and only thing that is vital between us."

—DIETRICH BONHOEFFER 36

"Community has made such a difference in my walk with Jesus. They believed for me when I barely had faith for myself." – Ashley

"At youth, I was able to say my struggles out loud — and my leaders stood with me. That's when I found true brotherhood." – Eric

"Community showed me the love of Jesus and keeps me accountable when I'm wrong." – Derek

"Youth was the first place I felt like I wasn't alone. It was like the Acts 4 church — fellowship that changed everything." – Grace

One Father's Day, a student without a dad called me to say, 'Happy Father's Day.' He told me I was the closest thing to a father he'd ever had. That moment broke me — and reminded me why this matters."
– Jake

Chapter 8

The Lies of Loneliness

"God places the lonely in families; He sets the prisoners free and gives them joy." Psalm 68:6

Big Idea: Loneliness lies—God designed us to be known, not just surrounded.

FOCUS ON THE ROOTS

On the California coastline stand some of Earth's most majestic living organisms—the mighty redwoods. These towering giants, some as tall as 300 feet, have survived storms, fires, and floods for centuries. But their strength does not come from their height or size, but from their roots. Beneath the ground, redwood roots extend outward, intertwining with the roots of other trees. This network forms a durable foundation, enabling the trees to stand firm against even the fiercest winds.

Like the redwoods, humans were designed for connection. Our strength lies not in isolation, but in community. Yet, loneliness has become an epidemic today, leaving many feelings disconnected and unsupported. We are tempted to believe that living alone is safer and simpler. However, as Elijah's story in 1 Kings 19 shows, isolation can lead to despair, while connection brings renewal and purpose.

Loneliness is one of the loudest voices shaping this generation and it does not just affect students. It affects leaders too.

The lie of loneliness is not that no one is around. It is that no one understands, no one sees you, and no one would notice if you disappeared.

And when that lie goes unchallenged, it slowly erodes faith, identity, and community.

For youth leaders, parents, and teachers, the loneliness epidemic is not just a statistic—it is a reality we see in the eyes of the students we serve. The challenge before us is not just to tell them about community but to show them how to live in it.

THE TRAP OF LONELINESS

Loneliness whispers lies that distort our sense of reality, convincing us that isolation is safer than connection. These lies grow louder the longer we stay alone, making us believe that stepping back into community is impossible or unnecessary. Elijah, one of the greatest prophets in Scripture, faced this same battle.

After a miraculous victory over the prophets of Baal, Elijah found himself running for his life. Jezebel's threat sent him into the wilderness, where he isolated himself under a broom tree and begged God to take his life. He believed he was the only one who still served God, that no one cared about him, and that his absence would not matter. These lies are the same ones we often believe when loneliness takes hold.

Loneliness often speaks in lies:

- You are the only one struggling.

- Everyone else has it figured out.

- If you were truly known, you'd be rejected.

- Isolation is safer than vulnerability.

Loneliness is more than just an emotional state; it is a silent epidemic with devastating effects. Research reveals that loneliness is as dangerous to physical health as smoking 15 cigarettes a day. It increases the risk of depression, anxiety, sleep disorders, and even premature death.

For Gen Z and Alpha, the problem is compounded by their digital upbringing. They have grown up immersed in social media, where relationships are curated, filtered, and transactional. This constant exposure to surface-level connections has left many of them feeling isolated, even in a crowd.

The irony is that God designed us for connection. The first problem in the Bible was not sin—it was solitude. In Genesis 2:18, God declared, "It is not good for the man to be alone." From the very beginning, we were created to live in relationship—with God and with one another.

Yet, many young people today are trapped in caves of loneliness, believing lies that keep them isolated and confined.

What are the lies loneliness tells us?

Lie #1: No One Will Miss Me

Elijah, one of the greatest prophets in Scripture, faced this same lie. After his dramatic victory over the prophets of Baal, Elijah fled into the wilderness, terrified by Jezebel's threats. Alone and afraid, he cried out to God, "Take my life; I am no better than my ancestors" (1 Kings 19:4).

Elijah believed his absence would not matter; he thought his life had no significance. However, the truth was that his role as a leader was critical. Without him, the people of Israel risked falling back into idol worship.

Young people often wrestle with this same false narrative. They may think, "If I skip church, will anyone even notice? If I disappear from this group, does it even matter?" But their presence does matter. For every young person who feels unseen, there is a community waiting for their voice, their gifts, and their story.

As leaders, it is our job to remind them of this truth: You matter. Your presence makes a difference.

Lie #2: No One Cares About Me

Elijah's journey did not end in the wilderness. He retreated to a cave, convinced he was utterly alone when God asked, "What are you doing here, Elijah?" the prophet replied with despair: "I am the only one left, and now they are trying to kill me too" (1 Kings 19:10).

Elijah exaggerated his situation because isolation distorts one's perception of reality. When we are alone, minor problems feel insurmountable, and we begin to believe no one cares. But even in his isolation, God cared deeply for Elijah. He met him in the cave, providing food, water, and reassurance.

For Gen Z and Alpha, feelings of being unloved or uncared for often stem from a lack of authentic relationships. They may have hundreds of followers online, but few people truly know them. This is where the Church has a unique opportunity to step in. By creating spaces where students feel seen and valued, we can counter the lie that no one cares.

Lie #3: No One Really Loves Me

The final lie of loneliness is the most damaging: the belief that we are unlovable. Elijah felt this acutely, but God met him with a gentle whisper, not in the dramatic wind, earthquake, or fire. The whisper was not just a demonstration of God's presence—it was an invitation to draw close.

Young people today are desperate for that same closeness. They need to hear the whisper of God's love through the voices of leaders, mentors, and peers who reflect His heart. And as we point them to Jesus, we remind them of the ultimate truth: "Greater love has no one than this, that someone lay down his life for his friends" (John 15:13).

LEADING THE NEXT GENERATION OUT OF ISOLATION

Isolation is rarely accidental. Scripture consistently shows that the enemy works in isolation, while God forms people in community. When leaders or students begin to pull away, it is not just a relational issue it is a spiritual one. Left unchecked, isolation becomes a breeding ground for shame, temptation, and despair.

As leaders, our mission is to help young people move from isolation into community. This starts with addressing the lies they believe and replacing them with truth:

1. Model Vulnerability

Let us recall what we learned in Chapter 1 students will not open up unless they see us doing the same. Share your struggles, your doubts, and how God has met you in moments of loneliness. Gen Z and Alpha crave authenticity. They are quick to spot hypocrisy and are drawn to leaders who live out what they preach. As leaders, we must model what it means to base our identity in Christ, rather than in our roles or achievements. When they see us finding security in Jesus, even in the face of criticism or failure, it allows them to do the same.

2. Create Spaces for Connection

Programs and events are essential, but authentic relationships are built in small, intentional spaces. Encourage small groups, mentorships, and one-on-one conversations.

> **"Leaders do not fight loneliness with better events they fight it with presence."**

Leaders do not fight loneliness with better events they fight it with presence. Consistency, intentionality, and follow-through matter more than programming. A text returned. A name remembered. A chair noticed when it is empty. These small acts create spaces where isolation loses its grip.

3. Show Them Their Value

Celebrate their unique gifts and contributions. Help them see how their presence enriches the community.

4. Teach Them to Serve

One of the best ways to combat loneliness is to serve others. When students focus outward, they find purpose and connection.

OUT OF THE CAVE

Elijah was not meant to stay in the cave, and neither are the young people we serve. God called Elijah out, reminding him of his purpose and surrounding him with others who shared his mission.

In the same way, we must call Gen Z and Alpha out of isolation and into the family of God. The Church is uniquely equipped to be the place where they experience true belonging, built on the love of Christ and the connection of His people.

Loneliness may be a growing epidemic, but it is not the final word. God's design for community is stronger than the lies of loneliness. Together, we can help the next generation step into the joy and purpose of being fully known and fully loved.

Loneliness loses its power when it is brought into the light. And the church was never meant to be a place people attend it was meant to be a family people belong to. If we want to lead the next generation well, we must be leaders who refuse to overlook the isolated, who pursue the unseen, and who create communities where no one must suffer alone.

REFLECTION QUESTIONS

When have I felt alone even while surrounded by people?

What lies about myself do I believe when I'm isolated?

How does loneliness impact my leadership?

What fears keep me from letting others in?

Where has God tried to use community to heal me?

———

Chapter 9

Finding Identity in Community

"I have been crucified with Christ. It is no longer I who live, but Christ who lives in me." Galatians 2:20

Big Idea: Identity grows in community because God uses people to reveal who we truly are.

A LOST SENSE OF SELF

A few years ago, Todd Davis, the CEO of LifeLock, launched an audacious advertising campaign. Confident in his company's ability to protect against identity theft, he boldly displayed his social security number on billboards, commercials, and even the side of trucks.

The stunt backfired spectacularly. Todd's identity was stolen multiple times, resulting in fraudulent loans, accounts, and thousands of dollars in debt. Ironically, the one thing he thought was secure was taken from him—because he gave it away so freely.[37]

This story mirrors the identity crisis so many of us face. While most people are not posting their social security numbers, they are still handing over their identities—often unknowingly—to people, possessions, performance, or popularity. For Gen Z and Alpha, this crisis runs even deeper. Growing up in a world of curated social media feeds, relentless comparison, and shifting cultural norms, they are bombarded with conflicting messages about who they are and what defines their worth.

This generation is constantly told to "find themselves." But Scripture tells a different story identity is not discovered in isolation; it is formed in community.

Who we become is deeply shaped by who we walk with. And when community is absent, identity becomes fragile, confused, and easily shaken.

As leaders, our calling is not just to tell young people who they are it is to guide them into a community where their true identity can flourish in Christ.

THE IDENTITY CRISIS

Everyone, at some point, wrestles with questions like:

- Who am I?

- Does my life matter?

- Am I loved? Am I significant?

However, for Gen Z and Alpha, these questions are amplified by a culture that associates identity with things that do not last. Dale Kuehne, author of Sex and the iWorld: Rethinking Relationship Beyond an Age of Individualism, observes: "Modern culture has created a vacuum of purpose and identity. This has led to colossal confusion over why we exist and where we find meaning."[38]

When identity is rooted in the wrong things, it inevitably leads to insecurity, confusion, and a sense of loneliness. Consider these common sources of misplaced identity:

1. Performance (I am what I do)

From academics to athletics, students feel pressured to achieve. But what happens when they fail?

2. Possessions (I am what I have)

Materialism becomes a measure of worth, yet possessions can be taken away.

3. Pleasure (I am what I want)

Culture elevates desires and feelings above all else, but basing identity on fleeting pleasures leads to emptiness.

4. Popularity (I am what others think of me)

Social media reinforces the lie that our value is tied to likes, followers, and comments.

Each of these identities is fragile, easily stripped away, leaving young people wondering who they are when the external markers vanish.

JESUS AND THE SEARCH FOR IDENTITY

The story of Jesus' baptism offers profound insight into identity. In Matthew 3:16-17, as Jesus comes out of the water, a voice from heaven declares: "This is my Son, whom I love; with him I am well pleased."

Before Jesus performed a single miracle or preached a single sermon, God affirmed His identity. He did not earn it through performance—He received it from the Father. This moment shaped the rest of Jesus' ministry.

But Satan was not content to let that identity stand unchallenged. In the wilderness, he tempted Jesus with conditional statements: "If you are the Son of God…" (Matthew 4:3). Satan's goal was to make Jesus question His identity and prove His worth through performance.

This same strategy is still in effect today. The enemy whispers lies to Gen Z and Alpha, tempting them to define themselves by what they do, what they have, or how others perceive them.

Our role as leaders is to remind them of the truth: Their identity is not achieved—it is received. It is rooted in Christ, not culture.

HELPING YOUNG PEOPLE FIND IDENTITY IN COMMUNITY

Loneliness worsens the identity crisis. Without community, young people are left to wrestle with these questions alone, often turning to unhealthy or destructive sources for validation. The Church, however, offers a unique solution: a family where they can discover who they are in Christ.

1. Affirm Their Identity in Christ

Like the Father affirmed Jesus, we must speak life over young people. Remind them:

- They are God's beloved children, created in His image (Genesis 1:27).

- Their worth is intrinsic, not tied to performance or popularity (Ephesians 2:10).

Words have power. When leaders consistently affirm students' God-given identity, it combats the lies they hear from culture.

2. Foster Relationships Over Programs

Programs are important, but they cannot replace relationships. Young people need safe spaces where they can be vulnerable, ask questions, and grow. Small groups, mentorships, and one-on-one conversations are crucial for helping them process their identity in Christ.

"Young people need safe spaces where they can be vulnerable, ask questions, and grow."

The early Church thrived because of its relational nature. In Acts 2:42-47, believers met daily, shared life, and supported one another. This kind of community is what young people need today—a family where they can belong and be known.

BUILDING A CULTURE THAT REFLECTS CHRIST

To help Gen Z and Alpha discover their true identity, the Church must create a culture that reflects Christ. Leaders shape identity by the culture they allow. The stories they celebrate, the behaviors they correct, and the voices they platform all communicate what truly matters. Community does not just gather people — it forms them.

This means:

1. Welcoming Diversity: God's family is beautifully diverse, and every individual brings unique value to the community. Celebrate differences while affirming unity in Christ.

2. Prioritizing Grace Over Perfection: Students need to know they are loved, even when they fall short. A culture of grace allows them to grow without fear of rejection.

3. Encouraging Purposeful Living: Identity is not just about who we are but why we exist. Help students see how their identity in Christ equips them to make an eternal impact.

ROOTED IN HIM

As leaders, we are called to guide Gen Z and Alpha out of the chaos of culture and into the clarity of Christ. Their identity is not found in what they do, what they have, or how others see them—it is found in the One who created them.

Like the redwoods, young people grow strong when their roots intertwine with others in a Christ-centered community. Together, we can create spaces where they feel seen, valued, and secure in their identity as children of God.

When young people know who they are in Christ, they not only thrive individually but become the kind of leaders who draw others into the family of God.

Identity rooted in community is resilient. It is not shaken by comparison or crushed by failure, because it is reinforced by truth and relationship. If we want to lead the next generation well, we must build communities where identity is formed in Christ, affirmed in relationship, and strengthened over time.

"When young people know who they are in Christ, they not only thrive individually but become the kind of leaders who draw others into the family of God."

REFLECTION QUESTIONS

Who is one person I can encourage with truth this week?

What can I do to create belonging in my ministry or home?

How does belonging impact my confidence?

What part of my identity is God currently redefining?

Chapter 10

More Than a Mentor

"Follow my example, as I follow the example of Christ."
1 Corinthians 11:1 NIV

Big Idea: Mentorship is not about giving advice—it is about giving your life away.

WHERE DO I BELONG?

Mentorship is often reduced to meetings, advice, or programs. But the most influential mentors in our lives rarely sat us down with a plan — they walked with us through real life.

The next generation does not just need mentors who speak into their lives. They need leaders who are willing to live alongside them.

I remember the first time I truly felt seen in church. After my parents' divorce, my mother began attending church with my sister, who found her way into the youth group and became a part of it. Seeing the positive change in my sister, my mother hoped for the same for me. However, I was not a fan of church at that time. I appreciated what it meant to my family, but I wanted no part in it.

I rebelled. I was angry and wished my mother would stop trying to get me involved. Whenever I attended, I would be the first to rush out as soon as the service ended, waiting in the car until it was time to leave. However, everything changed when some men from the church started reaching out to me. They discovered my passion for sports, especially football, and invited me to play at the church or in the park. The more I connected with them, the more my heart opened to church.

What began with sports blossomed into attending homeless outreach events with a men's small group, taking part in Bible studies, and eventually being part of the youth group, leading to my salvation at 17 at a youth camp.

These men mentored me and discipled me.

They did not just greet me; they took notice of me. They remembered my name, asked about my week, and invited me to share their table. It was not the youth pastor or worship leader—it was a group of older men who saw in me that I could not see in myself. Never discount the faithful men and women in your church. Those who do not need a title but lead world-class organizations. We need more unsung heroes in leadership.

That is when I realized: discipleship begins with a relationship, not just a Bible study.

For this generation, belonging does not stem from programming—it comes from genuine connections with people. While friendship is essential, it is not enough to sustain a relationship. Young people need mentors, coaches, and spiritual parents—individuals who walk alongside them, not because it is their job, but because they genuinely care.

THE ACHE FOR CONNECTION

We talk a lot about loneliness—and rightly so. But loneliness is not just the absence of people. It is the absence of a meaningful connection. And for Gen Z and Alpha, such a connection is rare.

According to Barna, more than 1 in 3 young people say they feel deeply alone. [39]Not just bored. Not just introverted. Alone. Many do not have an adult in their life who knows them beyond the surface. They have followers. They have friends. But they do not have family.

What they are longing for is someone to say: "You matter." "You're not too much." "You don't have to figure this out on your own."

When Jesus called the disciples, He did not hand them a workbook and wish them well. He invited them into His life. For three years, they ate, traveled, laughed, cried, learned, failed, and grew together.

They did not just get information. They got transformation through proximity.

Paul echoes this in 1 Thessalonians 2:8: "We loved you so much that we shared with you not only God's Good News but our own lives, too." (NLT)

That is mentorship. That is spiritual parenting. That is what we are called to offer.

> "When Jesus called the disciples, He did not hand them a workbook and wish them well. He invited them into His life."

We need to move from leadership language to family language. Mentors are not managers. Discipleship is not coaching. It is a relationship. And students do not just need leaders who are cool or relevant—they need consistent leaders.

Here is the truth: A small group can be biblical. A pizza night can be fun. However, if a student never has someone to turn to when they are in crisis, we have missed the point.

Students are shaped less by what leaders say and more by what leaders' model. How leaders handle conflict, pressure, failure, and faith forms students long before formal teaching ever does. Presence over time speaks louder than advice in a moment.

I am big advocate for power of presence. Presence means more than just showing up for official gatherings or scheduled meetings. It is about actively engaging in the lives of the students we mentor, being there in their everyday joys and challenges. True mentorship requires being present in all aspects of a young person's life, not just within the church walls. The power of presence is at the heart of lasting discipleship—it is felt beyond programs and sermons,

> "True mentorship requires being present in all aspects of a young person's life, not just within the church walls."

woven through real moments and relationships. Consider what it looks like to attend a student's football game, to stand in the crowd at their graduation, or to check in on them when they are feeling down. Presence is noticed when leaders extend their reach beyond church activities—when they remember birthdays or ask how things are going midweek.

As a senior boys' small group leader, I discovered that including the guys in everyday tasks—such as grocery shopping, filling up the car with gas, or helping clean the church—opened up space for authentic conversations and deeper connections. These moments were unlike our regular small group meetings, where we sat in a circle and followed a curriculum. Instead, we did life together.

Discipleship, in my experience, is more often caught than taught. Teaching is essential, but sharing everyday experiences made the greatest impact. For example, I remember one afternoon when we cleaned the church together. One of the boys began to share his struggles at school, revealing fears and frustrations he had not mentioned before. That simple, ordinary moment led to ongoing support and encouragement—not just from me, but from the rest of the group as well. Over time, I saw him grow into a confident leader, and today he serves the church with integrity and compassion.

Many of the young men I mentored are now serving in our local church in significant ways. Some are on staff; others have married and started families—a fact that makes me feel both proud and a little old! Reflecting on this, I am convinced that the lasting fruit came through the power of presence. Being present in their lives beyond formal gatherings allowed for genuine relationships to flourish, and those relationships became the foundation for their spiritual growth.

These experiences have also shaped me. Walking with these young men taught me about patience, vulnerability, and the importance of showing up, even when it is inconvenient or tiring. The lessons I learned from them have deepened my own faith and renewed my commitment to keep investing in others.

Presence is the heart of lasting discipleship. Sharing life's everyday moments—both the big and the small—is what truly matters, and it is through these genuine relationships that transformation takes root.

When our involvement is limited to the church, students may begin to believe that their leaders only care about them during services or events. This narrow connection can lead to feelings of isolation and the mistaken impression that they are valued only within a specific context. Leaders are not perfect, and everyone will fall short at times, but discipleship must extend beyond the four walls of the church to bear real fruit.

Leaders can make a meaningful difference by intentionally reaching out: send a quick message on a student's birthday, attend their extracurricular events, or check in during the week to ask how they are. These small gestures of presence convey care and support, fostering trust and laying the groundwork for deeper relationships.

By embracing presence in all areas of life, leaders become anchors of support, showing that mentorship is a relationship that goes far beyond formal settings.

Discipleship flows through a relationship. And a relationship takes time.

You do not have to be perfect to be a mentor. You just must be present. Here is what spiritual family looks like: It shows up, even when it is inconvenient. Even when you are tired, it listens. Not to fix, but to understand. It speaks the truth. In love. With patience. Without shame. It celebrates small wins. Growth is slow. Affirm every step. It keeps the door open even when students walk away.

STORIES OVER STRUCTURES

Creating a discipleship culture in your church or home is vital. Why? Well, for the simple fact that you will not remember the fifth sermon you preached last year. But you will remember the kid who opened for the first time. You will remember the moment a student asked if you could pray for their mom. You will remember when the quietest girl on your team started mentoring someone younger.

That is the fruit of a family. This is the joy of discipleship.

Programs are helpful. But stories are what shape culture. And every meaningful story in youth ministry begins with a person who chose to show up again and again.

You might be thinking: "This sounds great, but where do I start?"

Here is how: Ask God for eyes to see. Who is lonely? Who is drifting? Who is close, but hiding?

Start small. A conversation. A coffee. A "how can I pray for you?" Be interruptible. Mentorship rarely happens on your schedule. Invite others in. Teach your volunteers, parents, and older students how to do this as well.

Parents—you are the first spiritual mentors your kids will ever know. And the truth is, they do not need perfect parents. They need the present ones.

Model grace. Show up when you mess up. Invite others into your home. Let them see that following Jesus is not about having all the answers—it is about walking in faith, together.

The next generation does not need one more sermon. They need someone who will walk with them through theirs. They need more than leaders. They need a spiritual family.

So be the one who stays. Be the one who remembers. Be the one who says, "You belong."

The next generation does not need perfect mentors they need faithful ones. Leaders who are willing to stay, model Christ, and walk with students over time create impact that programs never could. Being more than a mentor is not about doing more it is about being present where God has placed you

REFLECTION QUESTIONS

*Who was a "spiritual family member" to you
growing up? What impact did they make?*

*Who in your ministry or classroom might be hungry
for more than just surface interaction?*

How can you model spiritual mentorship to your team or family?

*What might be stopping you from stepping into a
mentorship role—and how can you surrender that fear?*

Chapter 11

The Friend We Need

"A friend loves at all times, and a brother is born for a time of adversity."
Proverbs 17:17

Big Idea: The best leaders become the kind of friend they wish they had.

LET ME TELL YOU ABOUT MY (DAD'S) BEST FRIEND.

My dad is the most incredible man I know. He embodies kindness and serves as a living blueprint for what it means to be a great dad. I could continue praising the man he is and sharing what I have learned from being his son. One important lesson I have learned from watching my dad, who has been one of my role models for most of my life, is the value of being a good friend—a real friend.

The way I saw his interactions with his best friends, Luis "Louie" Jaramillo and Kenny Kendal, inspired me, and they continue to play a significant role in the friendships I aim to develop. Recently, Luis Jaramillo went home to be with the Lord. He had been battling a rare brain disease that slowly destroyed his body for close to five years. To know Louie was to see that he was the life of the party. Cracking jokes and sharing stories were his specialties. He had the rare gift of making everyone feel like his best friend with every conversation he had.

The day he passed away, I was able to visit him and say my goodbyes. Memories of our time together flooded my mind the moment I saw him. I remembered a trip from when I was around 9 or 10 years old, when my dad, Louie, and his cousins took their kids on a road trip to the Pro Football Hall of Fame in Canton, Ohio. Imagine a bunch of guys in a camper driving for days—it was wild! A trip I hope never to forget.

As all these memories flooded back to me, one thought I could not shake was that all the wonderful times spent with Louie resulted from his friendship with my dad. Reflecting on their bond, I realized it is rare to find friendships today that mirror my dads with Louie and Kenny.

My experience in ministry and living in the fast-paced environment of Miami has led me to believe that meaningful friendships have become a lost art. Many of the friendships I see today are based primarily on shared interests and hobbies, but they often lack deeper, more meaningful connections. I am not suggesting that you cannot have fun and enjoy everyday activities together; however, I have noticed that many friendships tend to fizzle out once the specific activity—be it video games or pickleball—ends.

True friendships require effort, especially in today's fast-paced world, where many things vie for our time and attention. The joy we share with our friends becomes even greater as we grow together in our faith through the Word of God, prayer, and being there for one another, even in the face of obstacles.

It strikes me that friendships like my dad's are becoming increasingly rare. You have noticed it too. We live in an age where we are more "connected" than ever—likes, comments, DMs, group chats—but many of us are still lonely. We scroll through highlight reels but struggle to find someone to call in the middle of the night. Social media gives us the illusion of closeness without the cost of commitment. Add to that the busyness of careers, parenting, and simply trying to keep up with life, and suddenly, deep friendship feels like a luxury we can no longer afford.

The kind of friendship my dad shared with Louie and Kenny was not built overnight. It was forged over decades—through shared meals, raising each other's kids, long-distance phone calls, and lots of laughter. It was not flashy. It was not always convenient. But it was faithful.

Looking back over the years, I have found some key points that I gleaned from my dad, which I hope will encourage you to become a master and recipient of true friendships.

The distance was never an excuse to disconnect.

Even when life pulled them into different states and seasons, they showed up for each other—sometimes in person, always in spirit.

Kenny became my father's friend when he left Cuba and found himself in Chicago. They played sports together and attended the same school, which strengthened their bond. However, their friendship was tested when my father moved from Chicago to Miami.

This was during a time when there were no phones or the internet. One might assume this would mark the end of their relationship, but they shared a deep friendship, and when you have that kind of connection, you find ways to make it work.

They wrote letters to each other, and whenever possible, they tried to visit one another as often as possible. Distance was not an excuse for disconnecting. Many of us have friends who live in the same city, have phones, or attend the same church, yet we still struggle to stay connected. I would challenge you not to let a lack of proximity or the comfort of convenience become a deterrent to supporting your friendships, no matter how busy life gets.

They helped raise each other's children.

There is something sacred about seeing your dad's best friend cheer you on as if you were his own. It taught me that real friends can expand the definition of what family means. Kenny and Louie played a crucial role in my football career, supporting me from Little League to college. Growing up, my dad and I would travel to Chicago every summer, and every trip included training sessions with Kenny. As an ex-college player, he was passionate about helping others improve and pushed me to reach my potential. I will always be grateful for those beach sand sprints on Lake Michigan.

I want the children of my closest friends to know me, and I want to have a meaningful role in their lives. I want to love them the way my dad's friends loved me, treating them as if they were my own. Whether it is offering wisdom now and then, saying a prayer, or sharing a funny story about their parents when they were younger, I want to create lasting memories filled with the silly moments we all experienced together.

They remained consistent, even in the midst of busyness.

Work, parenting, church—none of it kept them from checking in, showing up, or laughing over an old inside joke. Whenever I am in the car with my dad, there is a high chance that we are on the phone with Louie or Kenny. It was consistent.

Laughter was always close by.

Some of my favorite memories of my dad and his friends are the times I would laugh at the stories they shared about their youth. They recounted embarrassing moments from high school, their college antics, and even tales of how they took care of me when I was a baby. It was amazing to imagine them getting into trouble or pulling pranks on each other when they were younger. I could always count on Louie and Kenny for a good laugh.

Proverbs 17:22 says, "A cheerful heart is good medicine." Their joy was contagious. It reminded me that the best friendships are marked by lightness, even when life feels heavy.

And lastly, their friendship passed the test of time.

Ecclesiastes 4:9–10 says, "Two are better than one… If either of them falls down, one can help the other up."

Their loyalty repeatedly proved this to be true.

In a culture where friendships are often fleeting and superficial, we need more relationships like theirs—more people willing to go the distance, stay consistent, and love like brothers.

As I reflect on the legacy of Louie and the lifelong bond he shared with my dad, I am challenged to ask myself:

Am I the kind of friend who shows up when needed?

Do I pursue more depth or just convenience?

Am I building friendships that still matter 30 years from now?

We live in a world full of connections, yet we are starving for community. My dad and his friends gave me a glimpse of the kind of brotherhood that reflects the heart of Jesus, who did not just call us servants, but friends.

I am reminded that I do not just want to have great friends. I want to be one. Let us bring back the lost art of meaningful friendship, not just for the good times, but for all times.

For the young people in our lives, this kind of friendship is vital. They live in a world filled with challenges, pressures, and isolation. Gen Z and Alpha are often searching for someone to stand with them, to remind them they are not alone. As youth pastors, parents, and teachers, we cannot just hope they will find these relationships—we must model, teach, and foster them.

The next generation does not need leaders who are distant, but they also do not need leaders who blur the lines.

Students do not need another peer. They need someone willing to walk ahead of them, not just beside them. Being more than a friend is not about proximity it is about responsibility.

> **"The next generation does not need leaders who are distant, but they also do not need leaders who blur the lines."**

THE CONNECTION CONUNDRUM

C.S. Lewis once wrote, "Friendship is born at that moment when one person says to another, 'What! You, too? I thought I was the only one.'"[40]

That longing for connection resonates deeply with Gen Z and Alpha. Social media surrounds them with "friends," yet many feel isolated and unseen. Studies consistently show these generations are among the loneliest in history, despite being more "connected" than any previous group.

When leaders prioritize being liked over being trusted, formation suffers. Over-familiarity can erode authority, blur accountability, and weaken discipleship. Students do not need leaders who mirror their immaturity they need leaders who model what faithfulness looks like over time.

Being more than a friend looks like consistency, follow-up, honesty, and accountability. It means celebrating wins without enabling sin, listening without losing discernment, and staying present even when conversations are uncomfortable.

The challenge for leaders, parents, and mentors is clear: how do we help young people move beyond surface-level interactions to experience friendships that truly sustain them? The story of Jonathan and David in Scripture provides a robust roadmap for building these relationships.

THE FRIENDSHIP OF JONATHAN AND DAVID

In 1 Samuel 18, we see one of the most profound examples of friendship in the Bible. Jonathan, the son of King Saul, formed an unbreakable bond with David, the shepherd boy who would one day become king.

Their friendship was not built on convenience or shared hobbies—it was formed through loyalty, vulnerability, and mutual support. Jonathan gave David his robe, tunic, sword, bow, and belt. These were not just gifts; they were symbols of what real friendship requires.

Five Marks of True Friendship

In a sermon by Pastor Tim Ross, he discusses the friendship between Jonathan and David and reveals five essential qualities of a relationship that sustains and strengthens:[41]

1. Vulnerability: "Know Me."

Jonathan's robe symbolized his royal identity. By giving it to David, he was saying, "I want you to know me, not as the king's son, but as your friend."

For young people, vulnerability is the foundation of meaningful connection. But many hesitate to show their true selves, fearing judgment or rejection. As leaders and parents, we must model this first. Share your struggles, your doubts, and how God has worked in your life. Vulnerability invites trust, and trust is where friendships grow.

Create safe spaces for students to open up, such as small groups or one-on-one conversations.

2. Honesty: "See Me."

Jonathan's tunic represented transparency. He was not hiding behind his status or possessions—he allowed David to see him as he truly was.

Young people crave honesty. In a world filled with filters and curated personas, they are drawn to authenticity. But they also need help navigating relationships where honesty feels risky.

Celebrate authenticity in your own life and affirm it when you see it in others, especially in young people.

3. Protection: "Save Me."

By giving David his sword, Jonathan made a promise: "I will fight for you."

Real friends do not just stand beside you; they stand up for you. They defend you when others attack and remind you of your worth when the world tries to tear you down.

In 1947, Jackie Robinson broke baseball's color barrier, becoming the first African American to play in Major League Baseball. His journey was far from easy. Robinson faced relentless jeers from the crowd, hateful slurs, and even threats to his life. The weight of breaking barriers was often unbearable.

But in one unforgettable moment, his teammate Pee Wee Reese did something extraordinary. During a game in Cincinnati, as the crowd hurled insults at Robinson, Reese walked across the field and put his arm around Jackie's shoulder. The simple gesture silenced the crowd. More importantly, it told Robinson, "You're not alone."

That moment was not just about baseball; it was about friendship. Pee Wee Reese stood by Jackie Robinson in his time of greatest need, offering support, solidarity, and strength.[42]

The story of Jackie Robinson and Pee Wee Reese is a modern example of this kind of friendship. Reese did not just tolerate Robinson's struggles—he stepped into them. He used his influence to protect his teammate and to declare that Robinson was not alone.

Teach students the value of standing up for one another, especially when it is inconvenient or costly.

4. Closeness: "Be Near Me."

Jonathan's bow represented distance, yet by giving it to David, he closed the gap. He was not content with a surface-level connection; he wanted to walk closely with David.

Young people need friendships that are not just occasional but intentional. They need friends who will show up, listen, and walk with them through life's highs and lows.

Model intentional relationships by regularly checking in with students and encouraging them to do the same with their peers.

5. Support: "Lift Me."

Jonathan's belt held everything together. It symbolized support—a reminder that David did not have to carry the weight of his calling alone. Young people often feel the pressure to keep everything together. They need friends who will shoulder their burdens, stand with them in adversity, and remind them they are not alone.

Please encourage your child to seek out friendships where they give and receive support.

HELPING YOUNG PEOPLE BUILD LASTING FRIENDSHIPS

True friendship does not just happen—it is built intentionally. Here is how we can help Gen Z and Alpha cultivate these relationships:

1. Model Healthy Friendships: Let them see you investing in deep, Christ-centered relationships.

2. Create Opportunities for Connection: Plan events, small groups, or mentorship opportunities where students can build meaningful connections.

3. Teach Commitment: Help young people understand that real friendships require effort, sacrifice, and time.

POINTING TO THE ULTIMATE FRIEND

The story of Jonathan and David points us to Jesus, the friend who laid down His life for us. In John 15:13, Jesus says, "Greater love has no one than this: to lay down one's life for one's friends."

Jesus is not just a model of friendship; He is the friend every young person needs. When they meet His love, it transforms their belief of themselves and their relationships.

The next generation does not need leaders who try to fit in they need leaders who are willing to stand firm. Being more than a friend is not about closeness without direction; it is about presence with purpose. And when leaders embrace that responsibility, they create environments where students do not just feel known they grow.

REFLECTION QUESTIONS

How do my friends influence my spiritual direction?

Where has God asked me to be a better friend?

What friendships need strengthening—or boundaries?

What is one intentional way I can invest in a friendship this week

---

Chapter 12

Choose Your Friends Carefully

"Whoever walks with the wise becomes wise, but the companion of fools will suffer harm." Proverbs 13:20

Big Idea: Your friends shape your future—who you walk with determines who you become.

THE FRIEND THAT CHANGES EVERYTHING

The crowd inside the Olympic stadium was electric. It was 1936—Hitler's Olympics—and Jesse Owens, a Black American athlete, stepped onto the track carrying the weight of history on his shoulders. Nazi Germany wanted to prove their so-called racial superiority, and Owens was there to prove them wrong.

But in that moment, he was not just battling racism—he was battling his own self-doubt. He had fouled on his first two long jump attempts. One more miss, and he would be out.

Then, something unexpected happened.

Luz Long, a tall, blond, blue-eyed German—Owens' biggest competition—walked over to him. Instead of standing back, instead of hoping for Owens to fail, he leaned in. "You should be able to qualify with your eyes closed," he said with a smile. Then, he offered Owens a simple piece of advice: "Move your mark back a few inches to be safe."

Owens listened. On his next attempt, he soared past the qualifying mark. Later, he set a new Olympic record and won the gold medal. But the defining moment came after the jump.

In full view of Hitler and the world, Luz Long did not shake Owens' hand from a distance. He did not just nod politely. He ran to him and embraced him.

Years later, Owens said, "You could melt down all the medals and cups I have, and they wouldn't be a platting on the 24-carat friendship I felt for Luz Long."[43]

That is the power of the people we surround ourselves with. One voice. One moment of encouragement. One friend who changes everything.

I have heard it said we are one friend away from changing forever. So, here is the question this generation needs to answer: Are the friends in your life pushing you toward God's best, or pulling you away from it?

THE BIBLE'S WISDOM ON FRIENDSHIP

Proverbs 13:20 is a verse no one can outrun: "Whoever walks with the wise becomes wise, but the companion of fools will suffer harm."

We do not get to choose whether this principle applies to us. We only get to choose which side of it we end up on.

If you walk with wise people, you will become wise. If you walk with fools, you will suffer harm. It is that simple.

Jim Rohn once said, "You are the average of the five people you spend the most time with." If your closest friends are going nowhere, do not be surprised if you feel stuck, too.[44]

Young people need to understand this early. The people they surround themselves with today will shape the trajectory of their lives tomorrow.

HOW NOT TO CHOOSE FRIENDS

Josh Howerton, Pastor of LifePoint Church in Dallas, put it like this: Many of us choose friends based on two categories: Are they nice or are they mean? But that is not a biblical way to evaluate relationships. [45]

Some people are friendly, but they can also be dangerous individuals who will cheer you on all the way to destruction. Evil people can be really nice to you while leading you away from God.

At the same time, some people are rough but good people who challenge, correct, and even frustrate you, but ultimately help you grow.

Consider Nathan and David. Nathan did not tell David what he wanted to hear—he told him what he needed to hear, calling him out when he had fallen into sin. That is real friendship.

The friends you choose are not just a reflection of your present; they are shaping your future.

> **"The friends you choose are not just a reflection of your present; they are shaping your future."**

THREE TYPES OF PEOPLE IN YOUR LIFE

Proverbs 14:16-17 gives us a framework for the kinds of people we will meet:

1. **The Wise** – These are the people who lead you toward Christ. They bring wisdom, stability, and spiritual maturity into your life.

2. **The Foolish** – These are well-meaning people who make reckless decisions. They do not intentionally harm you, but their poor choices can pull you in the wrong direction.

3. **The Evil** – These are people who actively oppose truth. They manipulate, deceive, and cause destruction. Scripture warns us to be discerning about who we allow close to us.

The key is not to be judgmental but discerning. Jesus calls us to love all people, but our closest friendships should be with those who draw us closer to Him.

You Cannot Live the Right Life with the Wrong Friends

1 Corinthians 15:33 warns us: "Do not be deceived: 'Bad company ruins good morals.'"

Every young person believes they will be the exception. They think, "I'll influence my friends, not the other way around." But more often than not, it does not work that way.

The reality is simple: Your closest friends shape your faith.

That means students, parents, and youth pastors must take an active role in building friendships that reflect God's honor.

- For students: Choose friends who challenge and encourage you spiritually.

- For parents: Guide your children in forming Christ-centered friendships.

- For youth pastors: Create environments where deep, godly relationships can form.

THE FRIENDS THAT SHAPE YOUR FUTURE

Jesse Owens won four Olympic gold medals, but the thing that meant the most to him was not a medal—it was a friend.

One moment. One conversation. One friend stood with him. Your friends will either push you closer to God's purpose or pull you away from it. The choice is yours.

So, who is walking with you?

REFLECTION QUESTIONS

Who is profoundly influencing me—toward Jesus or away from Him?

Where have I underestimated the power of friendships?

What relationships drain my faith, and which strengthen it?

Have I ever ignored red flags in a friendship?

PART 3

CULTURE

"You never have to advertise a fire. Everyone comes
running when there's a fire. Likewise, if your
church is on fire, you will not have to advertise
it. The community will already know it."

—LEONARD RAVENHILL 46

"I was far from God until a friend invited me to youth. That one moment changed everything." – Eric

"What started as a small group turned into a ministry of 300+ young adults. Revival broke out, and God was in every detail." – Grace

"One of my students threw her vapes in the trash the same night she encountered Jesus. She said she had never felt so free." – Ashely

"We weren't planning baptisms after service… but the Holy Spirit interrupted, and that young man walked out free." – Derek

Chapter 13

The Language of the House

Big Idea: Culture is not what we say on stage—it is what we repeat in every hallway, classroom, text thread, and group chat.

EVERY HOUSE HAS A TONE

Every house has a language spoken or unspoken. And over time, the language of a house shapes the behavior, beliefs, and expectations of everyone inside it.

Culture is not first formed by vision statements or values on a wall. It is formed by the words leaders repeat, tolerate, and celebrate.

Have you ever walked into someone's house and at once felt a sense of it? The volume was loud and full of laughter. Maybe it was quiet and tense. Maybe it smelled like fresh cookies—or like middle school boys. Whatever the case, every house has a tone. An atmosphere.

Church is no different.

The moment a student walks into your youth room, your hallway, your sanctuary—they are reading the room. They are not just listening to your sermon. They are feeling your tone. And that tone… is culture.

Culture is more than just a vibe. It is not just about brand colors or the songs we sing. Culture is the unspoken code of your ministry the values that people intuitively grasp, even if you have not explicitly told them.

Culture is created in two main ways: what you allow and what you repeat. Take a moment to reflect on that. You do not need to preach about something for it to shape your culture; you only need to tolerate it for long enough or repeat it often enough.

> **"Culture is created in two main ways: what you allow and what you repeat."**

Long before people understand the culture of a place, they learn its language. They listen to how leaders talk about faith, failure, students, and the church and they quickly learn what is normal, what is acceptable, and what is celebrated.

Coach Nick Saban emphasizes the importance of culture by focusing on clear, value-based principles, accountability, and a process-oriented approach to achieving excellence. Key aspects of his perspective include defining expectations, encouraging positive behaviors while penalizing negative ones, and the belief that "the things you permit define your culture." He also highlights that culture is shaped by the individuals on the team, making alignment with common standards and objectives crucial for success.

That is why Joshua could boldly declare in Joshua 24:15, "As for me and my house, we will serve the Lord." He was not just making a personal declaration—he was setting the tone for his household culture.

So, the question is: What are we repeating? What are students absorbing between the lines?

THE POWER OF LANGUAGE

One of the easiest ways to foster a strong culture is through the use of shared language. Language shapes how we think, how we act, and what we believe is possible.

The early church understood this. Acts 2 tells us that they were "devoted to the apostles' teaching and to fellowship, to the breaking of bread and to prayer" (v. 42). Their culture was not built on a stage—it was built on everyday rhythms, repeated language, and consistent behaviors. And Acts says, "They enjoyed the favor of all the people" (v.47). Culture was their witness.

Here are some examples of what the "language of the house" might sound like:

- "Jesus is the center of our church."

- "People are the heart of our church."

- "Generosity is the catalyst for our vision."

- "Excellence is the culture of our house."

- "Legacy is our commitment to the next generation."

These phrases are not just clever statements; they are culture-building. The more they are repeated, the more they contribute to the spiritual DNA of your ministry. These are the culture statements of my church, Calvary. In every meeting and conversation, I strive to embody these statements, not only through my words but also through my actions. I aim to lead by example, showing how our culture should manifest.

As a leader, I never want a volunteer to understand the culture better than I do. This is not a competition, but I believe that if the Lord has placed me in this position of leadership with the responsibility to pastor people, then I must lead the way. I am a follower only of one person, and that is Jesus. Therefore, if someone wants to see the culture of your church, classroom, or team, let them look no further than your life.

Paul modeled this when he told the Corinthian church, "Follow me as I follow Christ" (1 Cor. 11:1). In other words, culture is not taught; it is caught.

In our youth ministry, we often say: "We lead from the front." If we want our students to worship, we do not stand in the back waiting for them to catch on—we lift our hands first. Even when the room feels awkward or the students are not engaged, we demonstrate what whole-hearted worship looks like. Culture is not shaped by wishing students would follow—it is shaped when leaders lead the way.

Another phrase we live by: "No one sits alone." If a student walks into service and is sitting by themselves or wandering around unsure of where to go, we make it our mission to make them feel seen. We do not leave it to chance. Students may forget your sermon, but they will never forget whether or not they felt like they belonged.

Those two simple practices—leading from the front and ensuring no one is alone—have created a culture that our students now repeat. They have become part of the "language of our house."

CODE BLACK

I genuinely believe our church has a world-class culture. Now it is not the only place where I have learned about the power of culture. The beautiful thing about culture is that it serves as a universal language; you can see excellent culture anywhere. Take, for example, a restaurant, theme park, or hotel that you love—behind it lies a culture that was intentionally created through meticulous thought and vision. I am blessed to have been a part of the process of building our church culture at Calvary and seeing the fruits of that labor. Additionally, I have seen how a strong culture can affect leadership, particularly in the world of sports.

When I think about excellent culture in sports, teams like the New England Patriots and the Miami Heat come to mind. In these organizations, what happens off the field translates into success on the field, creating a championship-caliber environment. Sports have played a significant role in my life. During my time on my collegiate football team, I learned the importance of building leadership, teamwork, and accountability—values that I strive to emulate to this day.

Playing for Harding University changed my life. If you ever have the chance to visit Searcy, Arkansas, I highly recommend it; it is a beautiful town filled with wonderful people. Walking through the halls of the Bison football facility, one thing becomes clear: it is not just a football team; it is a brotherhood. Head Coach Paul Simmons, a man I greatly admire and from whom I learned so much, is building a culture centered around two words: Code Black.

During my time as a player, Code Black was everything. It became our identity and a way of life, both in the locker room and on the field. Before the start of my senior year, Coach Simmons provided every defensive player with a laminated sheet with eight statements that define Code Black. This was effectively our contract; a commitment we made to uphold each time we stepped onto the field. Here is what defined Code Black:

Code Black:

1. Honor God

2. Brotherhood before Self

3. Passion in All Things

4. Accountability

5. Focus

6. Warrior Mentality

7. Never Panic

8. Finish

Honor God: First and foremost, we are a team—a group of men who honor the Lord with our lives, both on and off the field. If God is our everything, we need to give our everything back to Him. Our jerseys may have "Harding" stitched on them, representing the university we play for, but the real person we play for is Christ! Without this core value, the others do not matter.

Brotherhood Before Self: We must cultivate a culture of "one team, one heartbeat," where the team's needs take precedence over individual needs. The goal is bigger than personal wants. A selfish culture is a ticking time bomb of division, especially when our mission is to build a church that represents God's way of life.

Passion in All Things: Passion is contagious. Body language matters. When people walk into your church, facilities, or classroom, what do they see and sense? Do they see individuals who genuinely love Jesus? Are there leaders passionate about building God's house?

Accountability: Pastor Craig Groeschel once said, "What you allow, you promote." [47]If being late to meetings is not part of our culture, yet leaders continue to arrive late without accountability, then we promote tardiness. Accountability is the glue that keeps our culture healthy and intact. I cannot stress this enough: you must hold yourself and others accountable.

Focus: Keep a mind and vision that is laser focused. Are your thoughts or schedule filled with ideas that do not align with your leadership vision? We need to be faithful with the tiny things to be ready for greater responsibilities.

Warrior Mentality: Leadership is not for the weak. The moment you have influence; you have eyes on your life. Your students, peers, and family are watching you. With influence comes praise, but also criticism—mostly criticism. How will you respond?

Never Panic: John 16:33 (NIV) states, "I have told you these things, so that in me you may have peace. In this world you will have trouble. But take heart! I have overcome the world." Jesus is with us. You have a power source like no other. When things get difficult, remember who is in the boat with you during the storm.

Finish: We all know that it is not how you start, but how you finish that truly matters. Finishing strong requires commitment and determination. My hope is that this book has inspired you and taught you how to be resilient for the long term. Let us aim not to win the sprint, but to triumph in the marathon.

These principles served as the language in every team meeting and practice. I learned that repetition produces results. If you want a culture that others talk about, you must use this language every single day. I saw our coaches embody these values and consistently remind us of them. Have you created a language for your ministry? What is the identity of the ministry you lead? What are the key ideas that need to stay at the forefront of the minds of those you lead?

WHY THIS MATTERS FOR GEN Z AND ALPHA

Younger generations are highly attuned to inauthenticity. They will not trust what you say if it does not align with what they see. You can have sound theology while still having a toxic youth room. You can host a packed worship night and still have students who feel unseen. This is why culture cannot be merely preached; it must be lived, modeled, and multiplied.

How to Create Culture That Sticks

Here is a simple framework for intentionally building culture:

1. Define It

Write down your top 3 to 5 values. Keep them short, memorable, and biblical.

2. Say It

Incorporate these values into team meetings, teaching moments, and even decor. Repetition builds recognition. Do not be afraid of over-communication—when your leaders are tired of hearing it, that is when your students are finally starting to absorb it.

3. Show It

Culture is not just communicated—it is caught through consistency. Let your leaders model it first. If you want your students to invite their friends to church, then you need to invite your friends as well. If you want your students to evangelize, when you are with your small group at a coffee shop, lead the way by starting a dialogue with the barista.

4. Correct It

If something does not reflect your culture, address it kindly but clearly. What you allow becomes your new standard. Pastor Craig Groeschel puts it this way: "What you allow, you promote." The moment you fail to address an offense that contradicts the culture of your house; you signal to leaders that it is acceptable. This suggests that our language is not supported by our actions.

5. Celebrate It

What you celebrate gets repeated. When someone embodies the culture, shares the story, and makes it visible. The quickest way to destroy a culture you are actively trying to build is to let criticism overshadow celebration.

> **"What you celebrate gets repeated."**

Do not just correct what's wrong, spotlight what is right. When someone embodies your culture, tell the story. Highlight it publicly. Please share it in the leader group chat. This reinforces values more powerfully than a dozen reminders.

BUILD WHAT YOU WANT THEM TO CARRY

At the end of the day, students do not just inherit your theology—they inherit your culture. If you want them to carry humility, you must model it. If you want them to value family, you need to speak about it. If you want them to walk in holiness, create space where it is the norm.

You do not need the perfect lights or the trendiest merchandise; you need a healthy environment.

So, build the house. Set the tone. Create a place where students feel seen, safe, and sent.

This is how culture is formed. This is how legacy begins. This is how the Church becomes a home.

REFLECTION QUESTIONS

What do students currently feel when they walk into your space?

*What is one phrase or principle that could become
part of your ministry's shared language?*

*Are there attitudes or behaviors you have been tolerating
that are shaping culture in the wrong direction?*

*What is one thing you can do this week to
reinforce a value worth multiplying?*

Chapter 14

Becoming Peacemakers in Leadership

"Blessed are the peacemakers, for they shall be called sons of God."
Matthew 5:9

Big Idea: Culture drifts when leaders are not watching—what you tolerate eventually becomes what you teach.

BRACES AND CONFLICT

Anyone who has worn braces knows they are not exactly comfortable. They press, tug, and sometimes ache. Yet, behind that discomfort is a greater purpose: aligning things and creating lasting harmony.

In many ways, we as leaders are like braces—called to guide our teams toward unity, even when it means stepping into challenging, awkward, or painful situations. Just as braces gradually align teeth despite discomfort, our efforts as peacemakers may feel challenging but ultimately bring lasting harmony to our teams.

Conflict is inevitable, even among the most passionate and well-meaning teams. For instance, disagreements over event planning or differences in communication styles can quickly escalate if not addressed constructively. We have all seen how something small—maybe two volunteers who clash over their approach to organizing a retreat—can ripple out and affect the whole group.

But how we choose to handle these moments truly matters. If we avoid conflict, we risk allowing division to grow; if we face it with empathy and wisdom, we help foster a culture where trust and unity flourish. As we reflect on our own leadership, let us remember we are in this together—learning, growing, and sometimes feeling the "tightness" that comes with necessary change, all for the sake of deeper connection and peace.

THE COST OF UNRESOLVED CONFLICT

Let us face it: many of us would rather avoid conflict than confront it. We tell ourselves things like, "If I ignore the issue, it'll go away," or "I'll just keep praying about it and hope for the best." However, the truth is that avoiding conflict does not necessarily resolve it. It only makes things worse.

Unaddressed conflict does not disappear it multiplies. What leaders avoid today often resurfaces tomorrow with more damage, more emotion, and more confusion. Peacemakers understand that delaying hard conversations rarely protects people it usually prolongs harm.

"Unaddressed conflict does not disappear it multiplies."

Unresolved conflict does not just affect the individuals involved—it damages the entire culture of your ministry. It:

1. **Blocks Fellowship with God:** "If someone says, 'I love God,' but hates a fellow believer, that person is a liar..." (1 John 4:20). You cannot be right with God if you are wrong with others.

2. **Blocks Prayers:** Peter reminds us, "Treat your [spouse] as you should so your prayers will not be hindered" (1 Peter 3:7). The same principle applies to all relationships—broken relationships can hinder our spiritual lives.

3. **Blocks Joy:** James 3:18 says, "Peacemakers who sow in peace reap a harvest of righteousness." Without peace, it is hard to experience the joy that comes with healthy relationships.

Unresolved conflict is not just a personal or emotional issue—it is a spiritual one as well. And as leaders, we have a responsibility to address it head-on.

GOD'S CALL TO BE PEACEMAKERS

The Bible is filled with stories of conflict, but in every one of them, we see God's heart for reconciliation. From Joseph forgiving his brothers to Jesus' teaching about forgiveness, Scripture reminds us that no conflict is too big for God to resolve.

If God is the ultimate peacemaker, we are called to share His passion for unity and reconciliation. As leaders, we set the tone for our ministry's culture. When we pursue peace, we create an environment where others feel safe, valued, and heard.

> **"When we pursue peace, we create an environment where others feel safe, valued, and heard."**

Throughout this book, we have discussed how we model authenticity and vulnerability for this generation and the impact this has on them. There is no better opportunity to practice these traits than when dealing with conflict. If young people can implement this skill early in their lives, it will save them a great deal of heartache and help them avoid getting caught in a cycle of fractured relationships.

HOW TO HANDLE CONFLICT
FIVE STEPS TO PROTECT UNITY

Creating a healthy culture is not about avoiding conflict—it is about handling it with grace and wisdom. Here are five practical steps to address conflict in your team:

1. Be the First to Move

Jesus said, "If you are offering your gift at the altar and there remember that your brother has something against you, leave your gift… First be reconciled to your brother" (Matthew 5:23-24).

A few years ago, during one of our youth camps, we had a senior boys' basketball game against the leaders. These games were no joke; they were filled with a lot of trash talk, intensity, and testosterone. It is the most anticipated event of camp every year, with a lot on the line. As the game got underway, the intensity was palpable from the first dribble, with hard fouls and strong screens being thrown around.

I must admit that I am an extremely competitive person, and when things heat, my pride and competitive nature can get the best of me—and it did during this game. One of our students was playing physical defense against me, and as the match escalated, I reached my breaking point. My emotions got the better of me, leading me to push the student hard to the ground before trying a shot. I had to take myself out of the game. I felt hurt, embarrassed, and immature in front of the other leaders and students who were watching.

You would think that at camp, where the spirit of God was moving, I would have apologized in that moment, but I did not. Instead, that moment haunted me until one night at our church's prayer and worship night when the Holy Spirit prompted me to make things right.

Before worship started, I approached the student, apologized, and hugged him. The weight of guilt instantly lifted off my shoulders. I realized I should have been the first to make a move at camp, but I waited. Then I read this verse in Matthew 5 and realized I needed to make amends before joining in worship.

Reconciliation requires initiative. Do not wait for the other person to come to you—be the one to make the first move. Ignoring conflict only gives the enemy a foothold (Ephesians 4:26-27).

2. Beg for Wisdom

Before confronting someone, ask God for wisdom. James 1:5 promises, "If any of you lacks wisdom, let him ask God, who gives generously…" Pray for the right words and the right tone. Ask God to guide your approach so it fosters healing, not division.

In every conflict resolution meeting, I like to say a short prayer that goes something like this: "Holy Spirit, give me wisdom" or "Holy Spirit, help me." I often pray this right before the leader steps into my office or quietly under my breath when I know I need guidance in responding to what I am hearing. I recognize that I do not always possess the intellect or wisdom to provide the correct answers, and I aspire to have Solomon-like wisdom in these moments. This ensures that I do not hurt anyone's feelings or say something I will later regret.

Whenever you step into a meeting you know has the potential to go south, or you are dealing with a difficult person, do not leave wisdom behind.

3. Begin with Yourself

Conflict often arises from hurt feelings or misunderstandings. Before addressing the issue, examine your own heart. Are you acting out of pride or self-interest? Proverbs 13:10 reminds us, "Pride leads to conflict; those who take advice are wise."

Ask yourself: Am I seeking restoration, or am I just trying to prove I am right?

Our emotions can often lead us into trouble in ministry. It is essential not to take every adverse event personally, as doing so can make our hearts a place where bitterness can take root. Remember what we discussed in Chapter 1 about being self-aware. Sometimes we need to engage in self-reflection or seek guidance before scheduling a meeting or having a conversation when our feelings are hurt. While our feelings are valid, they should not be the primary reason for meeting with our leaders to address perceived personal attacks. In reality, most people are not thinking about us or plotting against us.

Do not walk into your church, office, or classroom and view everyone as your enemy. View them the way our Lord Jesus sees people. We are broken, sinful creatures in need of a savior. Just like us.

4. Start with Their Hurt

People do not just argue over ideas; they argue over emotions. As James 1:19 advises, we should be quick to listen, slow to speak, and slow to anger. It is important to try to understand the other person's perspective before jumping to conclusions.

In Philippians 2:4, we are encouraged to "look out… for the interests of others." Begin by addressing their feelings and concerns. This displays empathy and paves the way for healthy communication.

Whenever our leaders are in a conflict resolution meeting or need to hold someone accountable, I recommend that they ask three questions before addressing any offenses:

1. How are you?

2. How is your ministry doing?

3. How can I help?

These questions serve to calm emotions and remind us that we are in the business of reconciliation, not in the company of calling out or abusing power. I appreciate these questions because, by the time we reach the third one, the person often opens up, allowing us to work together to help them get back on the right track. This approach is far more effective than simply saying, "Okay, let's talk about why you are always late."

I am not suggesting we ignore the issues at hand; instead, we must shepherd people back to Christ. Often, there is a root cause for these surface-level problems.

5. Bring Truth with Kindness

"Speak the truth in love," Paul writes in Ephesians 4:15. How you say something matters just as much as what you say. Harsh words only escalate conflict, but kind and gentle words can bring healing (Proverbs 12:18).

As Max Lucado says, "Conflict is inevitable, but combat is optional."[48] The goal is not to win an argument—it is to preserve the relationship and protect the unity of your team.

RESOLVING CONFLICT, RESTORING CULTURE

Conflict does not have to destroy your ministry's culture. When handled biblically, it can strengthen relationships and deepen trust. Remember, God is the ultimate peacemaker, and He has given us everything we need to follow His example.

Creating a culture of unity starts with you. Be intentional about addressing conflict, seeking reconciliation, and modeling the grace and love of Christ. It is always more rewarding to resolve a conflict than to dissolve a relationship.

Cultures are shaped by how leaders handle conflict. When leaders choose courage over comfort and clarity over avoidance, peace becomes more than a feeling it becomes a foundation. If we want to lead the next generation well, we must become peacemakers who are willing to stand firm, speak truth, and pursue unity with wisdom.

> **"Cultures are shaped by how leaders handle conflict."**

Let us commit to protecting our teams, our ministries, and our culture by becoming peacemakers just as God has called us to be.

REFLECTION QUESTIONS

*What cultural issues have I ignored because
they were uncomfortable to address?*

Where has compromise begun to creep into our environment?

*How does my lifestyle reinforce—or contradict—
the culture I'm trying to build?*

What values have become unclear or misaligned?

Where is the enemy trying to distort or divide?

Chapter 15

No More Excuses

[16] Jesus replied: "A certain man was preparing a great banquet and invited many guests. [17] At the time of the banquet he sent his servant to tell those who had been invited, 'Come, for everything is now ready.' [18] "But they all alike began to make excuses. The first said, 'I have just bought a field, and I must go and see it. Please excuse me.' Luke 14: 16-18

Big Idea: Healthy culture attracts people—discipleship keeps them.

EXCUSES ARE EASY

Have you ever used an excuse to escape the consequences of a mistake? We have all tried to come up with excuses to get out of trouble at some point. One day, while exploring my iPad, I became curious about some of the craziest excuses people have given to their bosses, so I did a little research.

Experience.com and Businessinsider.com[49] conducted surveys among employees at various companies to find the weirdest excuses they could come up with. Here are a few of the most unusual ones: I was sprayed by a skunk; my bus broke down and robbers held me up; a hitman was looking for me; my brain went to sleep and I couldn't wake up; my monkey died; my cat unplugged my alarm; I had to ship my grandma's bones to India (note: she passed away 20 years ago); one employee said their uniform didn't fit, so they called in saying they were "fat"; another employee stated that her dog swallowed the car keys, and she was waiting for them to come out; I was spit on by a venomous snake; and one man claimed he broke his arm while wrestling a female bodybuilder.

The point is that everyone makes excuses. We often say things like, "I don't have time," "I do not feel ready," or "Someone else will do it."

But here is the big problem: excuses will always be there for you, while opportunities will not. I never want my excuses to get in the way of the open doors that God presents to me. I do not want to make excuses when God offers me a once-in-a-lifetime opportunity. Phrases like "Not today, God," "I will read another day," "I will show up next time," "God, I messed up," or "God, I'm ashamed" can hinder us from walking into the answers to our prayers.

> **"But here is the big problem: excuses will always be there for you, while opportunities will not."**

Excuses are easy because they give us an out. They feel safe. But excuses are dangerous because they delay obedience. And in the kingdom of God, delayed obedience is often disobedience.

Jesus knew the human tendency to make excuses, which is why He told one of His most urgent parables—the story of the great banquet in Luke 14.

THE BANQUET INVITATION (LUKE 14:15–24)

Jesus describes a man preparing a great feast and sending invitations out. Everything was ready. The table was set. The food was prepared. But when the servant went to call the guests, every one of them made an excuse.

One had bought a field. Another had bought oxen. Another had just gotten married. All legitimate-sounding reasons. But every excuse was really the same: "Not now."

So, the master became angry and told his servant: "Go out quickly into the streets and alleys of the town and bring in the poor, the crippled, the blind and the lame… Go out to the roads and country lanes and compel them to come in, so that my house will be full." (Luke 14:21–23)

The message is clear: God does not tolerate excuses when it comes to His invitation. The banquet is urgent. The house must be full.

EXCUSE CULTURE VS. KINGDOM CULTURE

Excuses do not just happen on the individual level—they become cultural. A church that tolerates excuses will slowly become a church that expects little, risks little, and changes little.

Excuse culture says, "Students won't show up if we challenge them." Kingdom culture says, "Students rise when you call them higher."

Excuse culture says, "Parents are too busy to disciple at home." Kingdom culture says: "Parents are the first pastors, and we'll equip them."

Excuse culture says: "We don't have the resources." Kingdom culture says, "If God has called us, He will provide."

Craig Groeschel often says, "If you want to change the direction of your ministry, change the excuses you're willing to accept."

BARRIERS VS. BRIDGES

Some excuses reveal legitimate barriers. Our role as leaders is not to dismiss them but to remove them.

If students say, "I don't know anyone," then leaders need to practice radical hospitality.

If parents say, "I don't know how to lead devotions," then churches need to provide resources.

If teens say, "Church feels irrelevant," then we need to show how Scripture speaks to their world.

We either accept excuses as barriers—or we turn them into bridges.

A STORY FROM MINISTRY: GO AND COMPEL

In our youth ministry, we decided to stop excusing apathy and start creating a sense of urgency. That meant shifting language: We started saying, "No one sits alone." Leaders intentionally scan the room, move toward students, and close the gaps of isolation. We say, "We lead from the front." If we want students to worship, we do not wait for them—we model it.

At first, it felt awkward. Students were not used to it. But over time, the culture shifted. Students began to repeat the language themselves. They started bringing their friends because they knew they would be welcomed and seen.

Culture changes when leaders stop excusing passivity and start compelling action.

FOR LEADERS, PARENTS, AND TEACHERS

Leaders: Stop excusing disengagement. Do not lower the bar. Call students higher. The gospel is worth urgency.

Parents: Stop excusing busyness. Your kids do not need a chauffeur—they need a shepherd. Prioritize faith conversations at home.

Teachers: Stop excusing silence. Ask the hard questions in class, open discussions, and create space for students to wrestle.

When leaders stop making excuses, those we lead stop making them too.

THE URGENCY OF THE HOUR

The master in Jesus' parable was not casual. He said, "Go out quickly." There was no time to waste. The urgency of the gospel is the same today.

Students are facing unprecedented pressures: mental health struggles, cultural confusion, digital overload. The house cannot wait until it is convenient. The invitation is now.

We must adopt the same urgency: Go out quickly. Compel them to come in. Fill the house.

The next generation does not need a church that explains why it cannot. They need a church that says, "We must."

No more excuses.

No more delay.

No more waiting for someone else.

Go. Invite. Compel. Build a culture that refuses to settle for empty seats when the King has commanded a full house.

Because at the end of the day, culture is not just what you preach—it is what you permit. And in the kingdom of God, excuses are not permitted.

In the end what we need to understand is that hope does not begin until excuses end. I like how Charles Spurgeon says it, "Excuses are curses, and when you have no excuses left there will be hope for you."

REFLECTION QUESTIONS

*What excuses have you caught yourself making
in leadership, parenting, or teaching?*

*How has your ministry (or home, or classroom)
unintentionally tolerated an "excuse culture"?*

*What practical step can you take this week to remove
barriers that keep students from saying yes to Jesus?*

*How can you personally model urgency in inviting,
compelling, and discipling others?*

Chapter 16

When Disciples Doubt

"Our doubts are traitors and make us lost the good we oft might win, by fearing to attempt." William Shakespeare

Big Idea: Doubt is not the enemy of faith—silence is.

BATTLES ON THE INSIDE

Louis Zamperini survived what should have killed him. He endured the brutality of World War II, months stranded on the Pacific Ocean in a life raft, and the horrors of Japanese prison camps. His story became famous because of the unimaginable suffering he endured on the outside—and the grit it took to survive

But what is often overlooked is what happened after the war. Back home, Louis wrestled with nightmares, addiction, rage, and despair. He had survived the battle outside, but the struggle inside nearly destroyed him. And that is a picture of doubt.[50]

You can survive the storms of life, fight the battles of culture, and even hold on through suffering—yet still feel undone by the quiet, gnawing questions in your soul.

That is where Thomas was. That is where many students are today. And that is where some of us, if we are honest, live more often than we admit.

THE DISCIPLE NOBODY TALKS ABOUT

Most of us can name Peter the bold, John the beloved, or Judas the betrayer when discussing the disciples. But Thomas? He gets remembered for one thing: doubt. For centuries, he has carried the label Doubting Thomas. But I want to suggest something different: Thomas is not the weak link of the twelve. He is a mirror. The Bible tells us that Thomas was called the Twin. But scholars have not determined who the Twin of was. You know who I believe he was the twin of? He is the twin of you and me. He is, as one theologian said, "the twin of us all."

Have you ever thought, "What if this spiritual stuff isn't real?" "I prayed about this, and God didn't show up." It can be scary and lonely in Christian circles or in church when you start to doubt. "Am I the only one?" "What will people think?" We feel wrong, guilty, and shameful…

Thomas's story reminds us of this truth: doubt does not disqualify you— it humanizes you.

> **"Thomas's story reminds us of this truth: doubt does not disqualify you— it humanizes you."**

Henry Drummond said, "Christ never failed to distinguish between doubt and unbelief. Doubt is can't believe. Unbelief is won't believe. Doubt is honesty. Unbelief is stubbornness. Doubt is looking for the light. Unbelief is content with the darkness."[51]

Thomas was not living in unbelief. He was wrestling with doubt. And that distinction matters.

THE SOURCES OF OUR DOUBT

Where does doubt come from? For Thomas and us, it often grows out of four places.

1. Personal Failure

Failure has a way of warping our perspective. Peter denied Jesus and nearly drowned in shame. Thomas may have felt similar. He had declared once in John 11, "Let us go and die with him!" But when the moment came, Thomas scattered like the rest. It is easy to wonder if doubt grows louder in the silence of regret. Many students today feel this. They mess up sexually, relapse into old habits, or fall short of expectations. And the whisper of the enemy is, "You failed. God's done with you."

But failure is not final with Jesus.

2. Lack of Understanding

Thomas wanted clarity. "Unless I see… I will not believe." He was not satisfied with secondhand reports. That was not arrogance—it was honesty.

Gen Z and Gen Alpha carry this same posture. They do not want clichés. They do not wish to receive shallow answers. They want authenticity, truth, and space to process. Doubt often surfaces when students do not understand—and no one gives them room to ask.

None of the disciples understood Jesus, no matter how often He told them about His death and resurrection. They pictured a conquering and reigning messiah, not a suffering and dying one.

Some of our doubts can stem from a lack of understanding of scripture, and sometimes, they result from a misunderstanding of God's ways.

3. Disappointment

Imagine the emotional letdown for Thomas. He believed Jesus was the Messiah—then watched Him die. Hope collapsed into grief. His fixation on Jesus' wounds may reveal how deeply it affected him. He could not get those gory details out of his mind.

Disappointment is one of the most fertile soils for doubt. A prayer unanswered. A parent walking out. A leader falling morally. When expectations crumble, faith feels shaky.

4. Isolation

Notice something in John 20: Thomas was not in the room the first time Jesus appeared to the disciples. He was alone.

Isolation amplifies doubt. When students disconnect from church, community, or mentors, their questions grow louder, and their faith weakens. That is why belonging matters so much—in community, we learn to see clearly again.

HOW JESUS MEETS DOUBT

John 20 gives us a stunning picture of how Jesus handles doubt.

1. He Still Shows Up

The first time Jesus appeared, Thomas was not there. Thomas was not in trouble for not being there, but he still missed out. There was a blessing for those who were there that he did not get. He missed seeing Jesus in the flesh, receiving the Holy Spirit, and hearing his new mission.

He had to go through a week of fear and unbelief when he could have been experiencing joy and peace! The other disciples kept telling him, "We have seen the Lord." This is funny if you have studied the Greek language. The verb used here is in the active tense, which means these guys were saying this repeatedly. Like my three-year-old daughter, who constantly asks, 'Why?' (parents understand this struggle)

Give Thomas, he returned up in the middle of his doubt. This moment reminds us of what Oswald Chambers says: "Doubt is not always a sign that a man is wrong; it may be a sign he is thinking."

But a week later, when Thomas was in the room, Jesus returned. He did not leave Thomas behind.

This is good news: even when doubt makes us withdraw, Jesus still comes after us.

2. He Invites Us Closer

Thomas refused to believe the testimony of many witnesses, his friends. He demanded extreme evidence, evidence of not only sight but also touch, and he repeatedly touched Jesus's wounds.

Here are some ways that we can ruin the blessing of being with Jesus:

- When we demand a voice, a vision, a revelation to prove our faith

- When we demand some exceptional circumstances to prove our faith

- When we demand an answer to every tricky question or objection

Let me warn you: there is a Difference between being desperate and demanding. AW Tozer says, "What comes to mind when we think about God is the most important thing about us."[52] In other words, be cautious in your approach to God.

Job 38:4 ESV reminds us of our small stature compared to the maker of the universe, 4 "Where were you when I laid the foundation of the earth? Tell me if you have understanding.

It will be hard to love God if our relationship is about His production instead of His presence.

Jesus did not shame Thomas; He welcomed his honesty! A disciple is not someone who never doubts; it is someone who lets Jesus transform their doubt into deeper devotion. J.C. Ryles puts it like this: "Doubting does not prove that a man has no faith, but only that his faith is small. And even when our faith is small, the Lord is ready to help us." [53]

Jesus does not shame Thomas. He does not say, "How dare you question me?" Instead, He says:

"Put your finger here; see my hands. Reach out your hand and put it into my side. Stop doubting and believe." (John 20:27)

Jesus met Thomas at the level of his questions. He showed His scars. He invited intimacy, not distance.

Students do not need leaders who panic at their doubts. They need leaders who, like Jesus, invite them closer.

3. He Transforms Us Through Encounter

Thomas' response is one of the most powerful confessions in all of Scripture: "My Lord and my God!" (John 20:28)

The doubter became the worshiper, and the skeptic became the confessor. One moment of honesty led to a lifetime of mission.

BUILDING A CULTURE THAT SHEPHERDS DOUBT

If Jesus responds to doubt with presence, scars, and invitation, our churches, families, and classrooms must do the same.

That means: Do not shame doubt. When students ask hard questions, affirm the courage it takes to voice them. Create safe spaces. Youth ministries should normalize Q&A nights, foster honest discussions in small groups, and promote open dialogue. Homes should allow kids to ask, "Why does God…?" without fear. Model honest faith. Leaders and parents should admit their own struggles. Students do not need perfect heroes; they need present guides.

When doubt is shamed, students leave. When doubt is shepherded, students grow.

"When doubt is shamed, students leave. When doubt is shepherded, students grow."

Thomas's story does not end in the upper room. Church history tells us he went on to carry the gospel to

India, where he planted churches and was eventually martyred for his faith.

The doubter became a missionary. The hesitant became the bold. The one who needed proof became willing to die for the truth.

And that is the invitation for this generation.

Your doubt does not disqualify you. It can deepen you. If leaders foster cultures of honesty and grace, then students will not hesitate to ask questions or walk away in silence. They will bring their doubts into the light—and find Jesus waiting with scars, love, and truth.

Doubt is not the enemy of faith—it is often the doorway to deeper faith. The next generation does not need a culture that pretends to have all the answers. They need a culture where they can bring their questions, see the scars of Christ, and confess with Thomas: "My Lord and my God."

Let us be leaders, parents, and teachers who refuse to shame doubt. Let us build churches and homes where honesty is welcomed, scars are shown, and faith is formed in the tension.

Because when doubt is met with grace, the next generation does not walk away. They rise—and lead the way.

REFLECTION QUESTIONS

Where do I need to create safer spaces for honesty?

How does Jesus model patience toward doubters?

*What conversation do I need to initiate
with a student who's struggling?*

What resource or teaching can I offer to address real questions?

Chapter 17

Share It Like You Mean It

"Look, I tell you, lift up your eyes, and see that the fields are white for harvest." John 4:35

Big Idea: The Gospel is too powerful to whisper—leaders must share it with boldness and clarity.

PASSION DRIVES SHARING

Think about the last time you discovered something amazing. Maybe it was a new TV show, a life-changing app, or even just a restaurant with the best burgers you have ever had. When you love something, you naturally want to share it. You bring it up in conversations, recommend it to your friends, and post about it online.

If you ask anyone in my church today what I am passionate about, they will tell you it is Walmart+. Yes, you heard that correctly, the grocery delivery service provided by one of the largest and wealthiest companies in the world, and I do not share in those profits. Here is the thing: Walmart+ has genuinely made a real difference for my family. Just last week, I saved $50 on groceries and avoided a long drive thanks to their free same-day delivery. The gas discounts have also helped us cut costs on every fill-up, making road trips and daily errands more affordable. We even enjoy complimentary access to Paramount+, which has added extra entertainment for our evenings together. Did I mention you get 25% off all Burger King digital orders? All these benefits—saving money, saving time, and adding value—have made our lives easier. Because it has helped us so much, I feel compelled to share it with others. If it can make someone else's life better, I want to make sure they know about it.

But here is the uncomfortable question: why isn't it as easy to share Jesus? If He is the most critical part of our lives—our Savior, Redeemer, and source of hope—why are we hesitant to talk about Him?

This chapter is not about guilt-tripping you into evangelism. It is about cultivating environments where young people naturally share their faith—not out of obligation, but out of love. Churches, homes, and ministries must model a passion for Jesus that is so authentic and contagious that it overflows into every conversation and relationship.

The reality is that we cannot help but talk about the things we love—whether it is sports, movies, a new significant other, music, or food. When you are passionate about something, it is easy to share. Lately, I find myself talking a lot about Walmart+. Anyone who knows me can attest that when someone mentions Walmart+ around me, I have a full sales pitch ready to go. I believe they should compensate me with a share of their billion-dollar revenue for every new sign-up I generate, as many people have started their Walmart+ subscriptions thanks to me.

The reason it is easy for me to rave about it is that I absolutely love it. Why? Because the benefits are excellent! Would you like to hear about them? Of course you do! The best part is that it saves me both money and trips to the store. With Walmart+, you get free same-day delivery for groceries, discounted gas prices, savings on auto care at any Walmart, and even a subscription to Paramount+ for free. New bonuses are added all the time—it is incredible!

If it has helped my family and me, why wouldn't I want to share this information with others? If it can be beneficial for someone else, I want to make sure they know about it.

A CHAIN REACTION OF FAITH

John 4 presents a powerful interaction between Jesus and a Samaritan woman. To summarize: while traveling through Samaria (which was unusual for a Jew), Jesus meets a Samaritan woman at a well and asks her for water. The woman is surprised by this encounter, considering the social boundaries of the time. Jesus offers her "living water," which, when consumed, leads to eternal life and satisfies spiritual thirst.

During their conversation, Jesus reveals that He knows her past—she has had five husbands and is currently living with someone who is not her husband. Recognizing Him as a prophet, she asks about the proper place for worship: Jerusalem or Samaria. Jesus responds by declaring that true worship is "in spirit and in truth," and is not tied to a specific location. He then boldly states, "I who speak to you am He," referring to Himself as the Messiah.

Astonished by this revelation, the woman leaves her water jar and goes to tell the people in her town, leading many Samaritans to believe in Jesus as the Savior of the world.

The story of the Samaritan woman at the well in John 4 serves as a masterclass in building relationships across cultural barriers. Jesus breaks many societal norms of His time by:

1. **Speaking to a Samaritan, a group that was despised by Jews.**

2. **Engaging with a woman, even though rabbis typically avoided women in public.**

3. **Acknowledging her past—her five marriages and current living situation—without passing judgment or condemnation.**

Jesus' approach was straightforward: He met her where she was, treated her with dignity, and spoke directly to her deepest needs. His love and authenticity broke through her barriers and transformed her life.

CREATING ENVIRONMENTS THAT REFLECT JESUS

The Samaritan woman's encounter with Jesus teaches us what it looks like to create spaces where young people can experience the Gospel for themselves. Here is how we can foster these environments in our churches, homes, and communities:

1. Be Real

We have already established this core truth. The first thing young people look for is authenticity. In a world filled with filters and curated personas, they yearn for something genuine. Jesus did not avoid the woman's past or sugarcoat the truth. Instead, He engaged her honestly and lovingly, showing her that she was fully seen and fully loved.

In our ministries and homes, we must model this exact authenticity. Share your own struggles and victories. Be honest about your journey with Jesus. When leaders are vulnerable, they create a culture where students feel safe to be vulnerable too.

2. Build Bridges, Not Barriers

Jesus did not let cultural norms or social barriers keep Him from engaging with the Samaritan woman. He actively broke down walls to show her that the Gospel is for everyone.

Similarly, our churches and homes must be places where all feel welcome, regardless of their background, doubts, or struggles. This means:

- Creating welcoming spaces where students can ask t tough questions.

- Teaching parents and leaders to respond to curiosity with grace, not judgment.

- Celebrating diversity in culture, thought, and experience as a reflection of God's creativity.

3. Teach the Power of Testimony

After her encounter with Jesus, the Samaritan woman did not wait to perfect her theology or clean up her past before sharing her story. She ran into town, leaving her water jar behind, and told everyone, "Come, see a man who told me all that I ever did. Can this be the Christ?"

Her vulnerability and passion sparked a chain reaction of faith. Despite her reputation, her testimony was compelling because it was real.

Young people today need to understand the power of their own stories. Encourage them to share how Jesus is working in their lives—not just on a stage, but in everyday conversations. Their testimony does not have to be polished; it just has to be honest.

> **"Their testimony does not have to be polished; it just has to be honest."**

THE CULTURE OF EVANGELISM

When we discuss creating culture, we are not just referring to physical spaces. Culture is the sum of what we celebrate, prioritize, and value as a community. If we want young people to share Jesus, we need to build environments that celebrate:

1. **Joyful Obedience:** Teach that sharing faith is not a burden; it is a joy. Just like the Samaritan woman, sharing Jesus should feel like an overflow of love, not an obligation.

2. **Relational Evangelism:** Equip students to share Jesus in the context of relationships. It is not about handing out tracts or debating theology—it is about inviting others into what God is doing in their lives.

3. **Eternal Impact:** Remind young people that their testimony can change lives. The Samaritan woman's story led an entire town to Jesus.

LESSONS FROM THE DISCIPLES

In contrast to the Samaritan woman's enthusiasm, the disciples missed an incredible opportunity. They went into the same town but did not share their faith. Instead, they focused on their physical needs—buying food—and assumed the people would not be interested in their message.

Jesus challenged their perspective, saying, "The fields are white for harvest." He reminded them that the opportunity to share the Gospel is always present, even in places that seem unwelcoming or unready

As leaders, parents, and teachers, we must challenge the assumptions that silence young people. Help them see every school, home, and hangout as a field ready for harvest.

When you look at your ministry, your family, or your community, what do you see? Do you see resistance, apathy, or disinterest? Or do you see opportunities for the Gospel to take root?

The Samaritan woman did not wait for perfect circumstances to share her story. She started where she was, with what she had. And God used her to transform her entire town.

Culture is not built overnight. It is created through intentionality, consistency, and faithfulness. When we model authentic faith, break down barriers, and empower young people to share their stories, we create environments where the Gospel can flourish.

Jesus did not just teach the Samaritan woman about living water; He gave it to her. In the same way, our churches, homes, and communities must be places where young people not only hear about Jesus but also encounter Him.

The chain reaction starts with us. Let us create the kind of culture that invites the next generation to not only accept Christ but share Him boldly with the world.

REFLECTION QUESTIONS

How does my lifestyle support or contradict the message I preach?

What excuses do I make when opportunities arise?

Who is one person I can intentionally share Jesus with this week?

What part of my testimony should I practice sharing more clearly?

———————

Chapter 18

Courage Under Fire

"Consecration is to a person and for a purpose … the process of consecration is cleansing plus sacrifice plus dedication equals consecration."
– Jon Tyson

Big Idea: We do not just need relevant leaders—we need consecrated ones. Students cannot stand firm in their culture if their leaders will not stand set apart.

WHEN THE CROWD DECIDES THE CALL

A study of professional soccer referees discovered something shocking. Over thousands of games, researchers noticed that referees were more likely to make calls in favor of the home team—especially in stadiums with loud, passionate, or even hostile fans. Even though these were trained professionals who were supposed to make unbiased decisions, the presence and pressure of the crowd began to influence their calls. The referees did not want to make the wrong call. But when the pressure was on, they were more likely to bend their judgment to please the home crowd.[54]

When I read that, I thought: That's not just soccer. That is culture.

Increasingly, it feels like we are refereeing in a packed stadium. Someone yells from the sideline whenever we teach God's Word or stand for truth. The pressure is real—online, in schools, even in churches. And whether you are a parent, pastor, or student, there is a temptation to adjust the call to avoid backlash.

But in a culture where everyone wants the leaders to "make the call their way," God is looking for people who will stand firm under fire.

Following Jesus has always required courage but the cost of discipleship is becoming more visible than ever.

We are forming the next generation in a world that pressures them to stay silent, blend in, and compromise convictions. Courage under fire is not a future problem it is a present reality.

THE PRESSURE TO COMPROMISE

David Wells says, "worldliness is what any particular culture does to make sin seem normal and righteousness seem strange"[55]

We have all felt it: pressure to tone down the truth so no one gets offended, the temptation to trade conviction for connection, and the fear of being labeled judgmental, out of touch, or irrelevant.

Culture is not subtle. It demands allegiance. It rewards compromise. And it punishes conviction.

But here is the hard truth: if we do not disciple this generation, culture will do it instead. And it will not do it subtly.

"Culture is not subtle. It demands allegiance. It rewards compromise. And it punishes conviction."

We are not raising students in peacetime—we are raising them in the midst of conflict. The question is not if they will be challenged—it is who will prepare them to respond with courage and clarity.

Cultures of courage are built when leaders:

- Speak truth clearly, even when it is uncomfortable

- Celebrate obedience more than outcomes

- Normalize faithfulness in small, unseen decisions

- Model repentance and conviction publicly

Fearless disciples are not formed by hype they are formed by consistency.

Let us go to Scripture: "In a large house there are articles not only of gold and silver, but also of wood and clay; some are for special purposes and some for common use. Those who cleanse themselves… will be instruments for special purposes, made holy, useful to the Master and prepared to do any good work." —2 Timothy 2:20–21

God is not just looking for talent. He is not just looking for charisma. He is looking for clean.

In a world where platforms impress, and production captivates, God is still searching for consecrated vessels—people who are set apart, purified, and available.

Why? Because you cannot be powerful in public if you are compromised in private.

Who does God use? He can use any personality, form of education, or background, but here is the key: you must be consecrated.

"In a world where platforms impress, and production captivates, God is still searching for consecrated vessels—people who are set apart, purified, and available."

Consecration: In the Bible, the word consecration is "the separation of oneself from things that are unclean, especially anything that would contaminate one's relationship with a perfect God."

I remember preparing the 2nd bedroom for Eden. When we 1st moved into our house, our 2nd bedroom was used for storage. It was just painted plain white. It was a mess. When we found out we were having a baby, we knew something had to change, especially our 2nd bedroom. We cleaned up, repainted, and prepared the room. We had to remove things, change things, dedicate time, and set things apart – to make something special for someone special. If this is for our child, it must be clean, and it must be the best because it is for our baby – this is what consecration looks like

Listen: You are made in the image of God for a special purpose. The greatest tragedy is that you are wasting your life on lesser things. You are the perfect vessel for God to use if you are consecrated.

When it comes to my faith, I will not apologize. I am not trying to be a regular pastor, husband, father, or person; I am trying to be used for a move of God.

God is looking for people to use for a revival in America, and he is saying, "Who can I use?" and that God would look at my life and say, "Phil has made himself ready."

1 Peter 3:12 NLT 12 The eyes of the Lord watch over those who do right, and his ears are open to their prayers. But the Lord turns his face against those who do evil."

CONSECRATION OVER COMPROMISE

Let us define it plainly: Consecration is the decision to be set apart for God's purposes.

It is not legalism. It is not perfection. It is saying, "I belong to Jesus—and I want everything in my life to reflect that."

And if we build a culture that changes students' lives, we need leaders who are more consecrated than clever and who love holiness more than hype.

Consecration is costly—but compromise will cost you more.

To experience God's power in your life through consecration, you need to know what consecration is and what it is not…

1- Consecration is romantic, not religious

We are consecrated to a person.

Titus 2:11-14 (NLT) 11 For the grace of God has been revealed, bringing salvation to all people. 12 We are instructed to turn from godless living and sinful pleasures. We should live in this evil world with wisdom, righteousness, and devotion to God, 13 while we look forward with hope to that wonderful day when the glory of our great God and Savior, Jesus Christ, will be revealed. 14 He gave His life to free us from every kind of sin, to cleanse us, and to make us His very own people, totally committed to doing good deeds.

1 Peter 2:9 (NLT) 9 But you are not like that; you are a chosen people. You are royal priests, a holy nation, God's very own possession. As a result, you can show others the goodness of God, for He called you out of darkness into His wonderful light.

What do these verses reveal to us? They show that God is a lover, not merely a moral policeman. Thus, consecration involves saying no to every other lover and giving our love solely to one person.

Before my wife and I got married, we went through an engagement period. When I decided to marry Dani and ask her to be my wife, I chose to say no to every other girl in the world and yes to her for the rest of my life. Her love was the only love I wanted. I had decided she was the one I wanted to be with. This is akin to being consecrated to the Lord, saying no to the things we once embraced. Why? Because I have decided to follow Jesus, and I will not turn back. I love Jesus because He first loved me. No love compares

2. Consecration Demands Boundaries, Not Living Unbound

We cannot live boundary-less lives. Where do I set my boundaries?

Exodus 19:10-13 (ESV): 10 The Lord said to Moses, "Go to the people and consecrate them today and tomorrow; let them wash their garments 11 and be ready for the third day. For on the third day, the Lord will come down on Mount Sinai in the sight of all the people. 12 You shall set limits for the people all around, saying, 'Take care not to go up into the mountain or touch the edge of it. Whoever touches the mountain shall be put to death. 13 No hand shall touch him, but he shall be stoned or shot; whether beast or man, he shall not live.' When the trumpet sounds a long blast, they shall come up to the mountain."

God sets the boundaries, you establish them, and you both enforce them. We are not at our best when we create our own boundaries. Who sets your boundaries?

"God sets the boundaries, you establish them, and you both enforce them."

You decide how many drinks you will have, how far is too far in your relationships, and what is healthy for you. Jesus is Lord; let Him set the boundaries.

3- Consecration gives power to the powerless

Reflecting on my hometown, Miami—known for its nightlife, wealth, drug culture, and social status—the foundation for God's revival power lies here. When that same dedication, if aimed at God, can generate true power. The passion you have for sports, anime, movies, and music should also be focused on God. Imagine what our ministries, teams, and lives would look like if we had the same zeal for eternal things that we do for temporary things.

God is saying, "Give me more room, and I will reward you with power." You already possess the spirit; you do not have to earn it; it is a gift. Can you be a person trusted with power?

God does not want to distribute more anointing to corrupt vessels. We need to teach our young people about the power and responsibility that come with living a life dedicated to God. When they experience His presence, they should crave it more than anything this world has to offer. It is our duty to show this generation the path of consecration—to desire a life with clean hands and pure hearts. This generation needs to understand that a life of holiness and repentance is nothing to fear.

In 1981, a Minnesota radio station shared a story about a stolen car in California. Police were conducting an intense search for the vehicle and the driver, even to the point of placing notices on local radio stations to find the thief. On the front seat of the stolen car sat a box of crackers that, unknown to the thief, were laced with poison. The car owner had planned to use the crackers as rat bait. Now, the police and the owner of the Volkswagen Bug were more concerned about catching the thief to save his life than about recovering the car. [56]Often, when we run from God, we feel it is to escape His punishment. But what we are doing is avoiding His rescue.

A CULTURE WORTH PASSING ON

If the next generation will resist compromise, it needs examples of those who have already rejected it.

They must hear: "No, I won't bend on that truth—even if it costs me influence." "Yes, I'm choosing purity—not because I have to, but because I'm free to." "Yes, I still believe Scripture is relevant—even when culture says it's outdated."

They need to see leaders live what they preach.

Culture forms students by what it normalizes. But the Church should form students by what it consecrates.

We do not just pass on messages—we pass on models. We do not just teach theology—we model integrity. We do not just post about revival—we live it.

There is a reason Scripture uses fire so often: Fire reveals what is real. Fire purifies what is impure. Fire strengthens what is surrendered. And the fire is here.

> **"Culture forms students by what it normalizes. But the Church should form students by what it consecrates."**

But here is the promise: "When you walk through the fire, you will not be burned; the flames will not set you ablaze."—Isaiah 43:2

Not because you are strong. But because He is with you. So, when students are mocked for their faith, stand with them. When culture demands silence, speak truth in love. When compromise is easy—choose consecration anyway. God is looking for vessels. Let us be the kind He can use.

Do not Just Survive the Fire—Shine in It

You were not called to blend in. You were called to stand out.

Culture is loud, but courage is more audible. When students see leaders live with integrity, boldness, and purity, they do not forget it.

We do not need trend-chasing youth ministries. We need fire-tested, Jesus-anchored movements.

So, consecrate yourself. Not to earn approval, but to carry His power. The next generation will rise not just because of what we say… but also because of how we stand.

Let us give them something worth following. Let us provide them with a culture worth carrying. Let us give them courage—under fire.

REFLECTION QUESTIONS

What areas of your life need to be re-consecrated to God?

*Where have you been tempted to compromise
truth to stay comfortable?*

*What would it look like to raise students
who are holy, not just hyped?*

*How can you build a culture that rewards
conviction instead of platform?*

Chapter 19

Faith That Stays

11 For no one can lay any foundation other than the one we already have—Jesus Christ. 12 Anyone who builds on that foundation may use a variety of materials—gold, silver, jewels, wood, hay, or straw. 13 But on the judgment day, fire will reveal what kind of work each builder has done. The fire will show if a person's work has any value.
- 1 Corinthians 3:11-13 NLT

Big Idea: Faithfulness is the correct measure of leadership—not how fast you start, but how long you stay.

THE POST-CAMP CRASH

I have seen this "movie" play out many times in my years serving students. It always starts the same way. The bus ride back from camp is filled with laughter, stories, and a sense of excitement. Students share how God had spoken to them, how their lives had been changed, and the commitments they had made to follow Jesus more closely. It is one of those mountaintop moments—when the presence of God feels so real, so tangible, that nothing seems impossible.

But then Monday came. School started again. The pressures of friends, homework, and social media crept back in. Slowly, the fire ignited at camp began to fade. By the time Sunday or Friday night rolled around, many of those same students had slipped back into old habits, wondering whether the transformation they felt was even fundamental.

This is the heartbreaking pattern many leaders' witnesses: young people meet Jesus in powerful ways, but when they return to the "real world," their faith begins to waver. The problem is not the camp or the confer-ence—it is the lack of a structure to sustain what God began.

I tell our team this: what happens at camp cannot stay at camp. The presence of God is not confined to the camp auditorium, waiting for us to return like a genie trapped in Aladdin's lamp. If we have the Holy Spirit within us, then, technically, camp goes with us wherever we go. The same type of worship we experience at a camp or conference can also be felt in the comfort of our homes or while driving home from work. We must be careful not to blur the lines between superstition and the supernatural.

As leaders, our challenge is clear: how do we create environments—churches, homes, and communities—where faith not only flickers but flourishes?

THE FOUNDATION MATTERS

Paul's words in 1 Corinthians 3:11-13 vividly portray what it means to build a lasting faith. He describes a foundation laid in Christ and warns that the materials we use to build upon it—gold, silver, wood, or straw—will be tested by fire.

Faith rooted in Jesus is unshakable, but what we build on that foundation determines whether it stands or falls when life gets hard. For young people, the mountaintop experience is like laying a foundation. It is a start, but it is not the whole structure. What happens next—the daily decisions, the habits formed, and the relationships cultivated—will either strengthen their faith or leave it vulnerable.

> **"Faith rooted in Jesus is unshakable, but what we build on that foundation determines whether it stands or falls when life gets hard."**

What are some practical ways we can cultivate a culture in our youth ministries, homes, or churches that will help us capitalize on the robust foundation laid when students encounter Jesus in a life-changing way? First, we must…

1. Build with the Holy Spirit, Not Hype

Hear me clearly: hype may get them in the room, but the spirit keeps them there. Camp experiences and conferences are often fueled by high-energy worship, passionate preaching, and an atmosphere charged with emotion. If you have ever attended a youth camp, you know exactly what I am talking about. Tears are not uncommon during these events. Only at a youth camp will you see middle schoolers, often lacking deodorant, wrapping their arms around each other and crying out to Jesus at the center. I like to think those tears are holy, but I often struggle with the thought that they might instead be due to the strong body odor wafting around them. This is something I wrestle with God about. But I digress. What I am trying to say is this. While these moments are valuable, emotions alone cannot sustain faith.

At camp, students may feel spirit filled. But when they return home, many unknowingly put the Holy Spirit on "do not disturb" until the next big event. The result? They live off hype, not the Helper. This is a problem, and poor theology, though not intentional, may be the cause. Have we taught our young people about the Holy Spirit? Who is he, and what does he do? The most important thing they need to grasp is that the Holy Spirit is not confined to camps or conferences. He is present in the everyday, ready to guide, comfort, and empower. Romans 8:26 reminds us, "The Holy Spirit helps us in our weakness."

How We Help Students:

- Teach them to seek the Holy Spirit in ordinary moments—before a test, during a difficult conversation, or when making decisions.

- Encourage regular prayer and Scripture reading as ways to stay connected to the Spirit.

Faith is not about living for the next emotional high; it is about walking daily with the God who never leaves. This is especially true for students, and it can be dangerous to their walk with Christ.

Now, I do not want to come across as a boomer who is anti-fun or high-energy, complaining that the music is too loud. If you were to ever step foot into our church on a Friday night for our youth service, it is wild in all the best ways possible. Students mosh to a praise song, shout down the preacher, and afterward play all kinds of sports. It is active, and I love it. However, remember that this is not the main win. Our energy and culture should complement what the Spirit is already doing in your midst and in the lives of your students.

The danger of emotionalism is that it can lead our students to live each day with a faith that is not battle-tested. When adversity strikes their lives, they lean on hype and realize it is not sustainable, leading them to doubt or unbelief. So, let us talk about emotions a bit more.

WHEN EMOTION IS NOT ENOUGH

Everyone loves going on vacation, a time to get away from work, the busyness of life, and everything else that stresses us. I recently discovered that vacations serve a purpose beyond just getting away; couples also use them to rekindle their love. A study I recently saw found that 42% of Americans have fallen back in love with a partner after going on vacation together.[57] Another survey of 2,000 adults examined the magic of vacationing and found that three-quarters of respondents believe vacations are great for those looking to keep the spark alive in their relationships. When on vacation with others, two-thirds of respondents tried to take as many photos as possible to commemorate the trip. Looking back at these pictures, they did so an average of five times throughout the year. [58] From relaxing on the beach to resort experiences, families, friends, or couples are bound to return from vacation with memories that will last a lifetime.

The question I have is: what happens when you come back? What happens when vacation is over?

The emotional high has subsided – the memories you made are starting to fade – the beautiful scenery is gone – the schedule of doing nothing has come to an end – The experience has ended, and we are back to reality….

We will say things like – "can't wait to go back" – "man, I wish I were at…" "I need another vacation, "if I can only get away."

Why? Because inside every one of us is a motivation to try and experience events that heighten our emotions, and when it ends, the need to repeat that experience stays with us

What would it look like if we had a vacation mindset for our Christian lifestyle?

What I mean is that if we are not careful, we can let our emotions and feelings drive us to crave experiences with Jesus instead of encounters with Jesus…

This is how many students experience faith.

They attend camp or a powerful conference, have an incredible emotional experience, raise their hands in worship, and may even cry. They feel God. They sense purpose. But then they come home—to conflict, temptation, doubt, and spiritual dryness. Within days, that encounter fades. – Why?

While emotional moments can mark us, they do not mature us. Emotion is a beautiful starting point, but it is not a sustainable foundation.

"While emotional moments can mark us, they do not mature us. Emotion is a beautiful starting point, but it is not a sustainable foundation."

We live in a time when many youth ministries unintentionally build faith on hype rather than on the Holy Spirit. We can rally a crowd, drop fog on the stage, and cue the drop in the worship set exactly right—but if we do not disciple students into the daily, ordinary, sometimes hard rhythm of walking with Jesus, their faith will not last beyond the weekend.

EMOTION IS GOOD—BUT NOT THE GOAL

I love emotion. I want students to experience joy, tears, and spiritual hunger. But there is a difference between being moved by God and being formed by Him.

"The spirit is willing, but the flesh is weak." —Matthew 26:41

Jesus said this to His disciples in the garden—not because they were bad, but because they were human. They had good intentions but lacked endurance. It is the same today. Many students are willing to follow Jesus—but if we do not train them in the rhythms of prayer, the Word, community, and obedience, they will quickly burn out.

Emotional faith is not bad. It is just incomplete.

When the Spirit Builds, It Lasts

Throughout Scripture, we see moments when people are tempted to pursue outward appearances rather than inward substance.

In Genesis, the people tried to build a tower to the heavens to make a name for themselves. It was tall, impressive, and ambitious. But the Spirit did not build it—it was built by pride. And it crumbled.

Then in Acts 2, we see the opposite. A group of nobodies in an upper room, praying and waiting on God. No lights. No hype. Just hunger. And when the Holy Spirit fell, that moment sparked the movement we now call the Church.

Man built one. The other by God.

"Unless the Lord builds the house, the builders labor in vain." —Psalm 127:1

SPIRIT-LED VS. HYPE-DRIVEN

Let us be clear: there is nothing wrong with creativity, energy, or excellence. But the goal is not to impress students. The goal is to form them in the image of Christ.

If we build ministries where students only experience God in emotional highs, they will constantly chase moments and miss the maturity that comes with it.

Genuine discipleship teaches them:

How to follow Jesus when it is boring

How to pray when God feels silent

How to stand firm when culture pushes back

How to trust truth over feelings

As Galatians 5:25 reminds us, "Since we live by the Spirit, let us keep in step with the Spirit."

It does not say "leap with the Spirit." It says step. Slow. Steady. Consistent.

Emotion fades. Hype dies. Yet when students are grounded in the Holy Spirit—when they have learned to walk with Him daily, not merely feel Him momentarily—they develop a faith that endures.

So, let us build ministries that help them endure, not just emote. Let us create rooms filled with God's presence, not just hype and energy. Let us help them build with the Spirit—because that is what lasts when the feelings fade.

2. Build Through Authentic Community

We have discussed this point extensively, particularly in relation to camps or events. The first week back after camp can be isolating for students, as they return to environments that often do not reflect the spiritual highs they experienced during their time away. This is why community is so crucial.

Consider that a youth camp typically lasts from three to seven days. During that time, students are surrounded by peers who pray for them, worship together, and read God's Word daily. When they return home, they are often thrust back into situations filled with temptation and into conversations they were not exposed to during camp.

Proverbs 27:17 says, "As iron sharpens iron, so one person sharpens another." Faith grows in fellowship. Young people need relationships with peers and mentors who encourage, challenge, and support them through prayer.

How We Help Students:

- Create small groups where students can share openly about their struggles and victories.

- Encourage them to surround themselves with friends who are walking with Jesus.

- Be intentional about follow-up after big events. Do not let the momentum die—fan the flame.

Community is not just a support system; it reflects God's design for the Church.

3. Cut Out Distractions

Distractions are everywhere—social media, peer pressure, and even seemingly good things compete for our attention. A great example of this can be found in the stories of Hank Aaron and Yogi Berra. As a catcher for the Yankees, Yogi was known for his trash talk. One of a catcher's roles is to distract the batter, so they often say offensive or irritating things to throw the player off their game.

On one occasion, when Hank Aaron came up to bat, Yogi started saying, "All right, Hank is getting ready to bat." Hank remained silent. Yogi continued, "Hank, you've got the writing on the bat in the wrong place. The words should be facing you." He was trying to get Hank to look at his bat to check its orientation. Yogi pressed further, "You better check it." Hank stayed focused and didn't respond.

After the next pitch, Hank hit a home run. As he rounded the bases and stepped on home plate, he walked toward the dugout. Then he stopped, turned back, looked at Yogi Berra, and said, "I didn't come here to read." [59]

Hank Aaron's response after hitting that home run serves as a powerful reminder to stay focused on our purpose, despite distractions designed to pull our attention away.

For young people, clarity about their purpose is essential when they understand why their faith matters, they are less likely to be swayed by the surrounding noise.

How We Help Students:

- Teach them to name distractions and set boundaries (e.g., limiting screen time, choosing their influences wisely).

- Remind them of their calling and purpose in Christ.

A focused faith is a resilient faith. Creating a Culture That Sustains Faith

The environments we create in our churches and homes must do more than inspire—they must equip. Here is how:

1. Prioritize Discipleship Over Events

Events spark change, but discipleship sustains it. Teach students how to study the Bible, pray, and share their faith. Equip them to grow independently, not just depend on programs.

2. Celebrate Small Wins

Faith is built step by step. Celebrate when a student starts a daily prayer routine, leads a small group, or shares their testimony. These moments reinforce the idea that growth is a process.

3. Involve Parents

Faith flourishes when it is nurtured at home. Equip parents to have faith-based conversations, model Christlike behavior, and create a home environment that reflects the love of Jesus.

FROM MOMENTS TO MOVEMENT

Mountaintop experiences are powerful, but they are only the beginning. For faith to last, it must move from a moment to a movement—a daily, intentional pursuit of Jesus.

Moments are not the mission. They are preparing for it.

THE TEMPTATION OF COMFORT (MATTHEW 17:1–4)

Peter, James, and John experienced one of the most remarkable spiritual encounters ever recorded. Jesus took them up a high mountain, and suddenly His face shone like the sun, and His clothes became dazzling white. Moses and Elijah appeared to join the conversation.

It is easy to follow Jesus on the mountain, but true faith is tested in the valley. There is a reason Jesus took Peter, James, and John up the mountain: to illustrate the power of separation and the importance of preparation.

If we want to see Jesus in His glory, we must often step away from the crowd. In that secluded spot, away from the noise, we can be alone with Jesus. We feel close to Jesus during retreats because, like Peter, James, and John, we set aside distractions and find a quiet place to focus on Him. We must learn to step away from the "norm" and ascend the hill alone or with trusted friends to spend time in His presence.

Charles Spurgeon once said, "The best visits from Christ are like the best visits we have from those we love—not in the busy market or on a crowded street, but when we are alone with Him."[60]

This separation leads to preparation...

JESUS AND THE TRANSFIGURATION (MATTHEW 7:2)

Transfigured = Metamorphosis. It refers to a change on the outside that originates from within. When a caterpillar constructs a cocoon and later appears as a butterfly, this transformation is due to metamorphosis. For Jesus, this change on the outside came from within.

Jesus is Transfigured — Not for Himself, but for His Disciples

This moment confirmed for Peter, James, and John that Jesus was indeed who He claimed to be, even when later challenges arose (such as His crucifixion). Jesus revealed His glory to them, pulling back the curtain so they would never forget who they were following, even when circumstances appeared bleak.

As N.T. Wright notes in *Matthew for Everyone,* "The mountain was the place where heaven and earth met for a moment — not to give the disciples a spiritual high, but to anchor them for what lay ahead."[61]

This was no ordinary moment; it was *the* moment. Peter then reacted in a way many of us might: "Lord, it is good for us to be here. If you wish, I will put up three shelters — one for you, one for Moses, and one for Elijah." (v. 4)

In other words, he wanted to stay there forever.

Peter intended to build a tent around this moment, but Jesus did not lead them up the mountain to stay there; He brought them there to prepare them for something else. This reflects our temptation as well. We often wish to freeze special moments, cling to feelings, and remain comfortable. While the mountain may feel safe, the mission lies in the valley.

Here is the truth: do not build a tent; build a life.

Who would not want to linger in such a moment? Peter proposed building three shrines for Jesus, Moses, and Elijah, yet what a self-centered thought that was— "Lord, it is good that we are here." What about the other twelve disciples? What about the rest of the world? Peter wanted to hold on to that moment, but God had a greater mission in mind.

Consider stagnant water. When water ceases to flow, it becomes stagnant — and what happens? It attracts mosquitoes, breeds bacteria, and begins to stink. Healthy water flows through rivers, streams, or even filters. Conversely, stagnant water becomes hazardous. Similarly, faith that stops moving turns toxic; it breeds doubt, apathy, and compromise. The instant you cease moving with Jesus, your soul begins to stagnate.

MOMENTS ARE PREPARATION, NOT DESTINATION

The Transfiguration was not primarily about Peter's comfort but about the disciples' calling. God was not saying, "Here's a great experience—enjoy it while it lasts." Instead, He proclaimed, "Here's who Jesus really is—now listen to Him."

"This is my Son, whom I love; with Him, I am well pleased. Listen to Him!" (v. 5)

Sometimes, the most significant barrier to listening to Jesus is our own inner voice.

Our chaotic self-talk needs to be interrupted—what a blessed interruption it is! We should thank God for stopping our incessant babbling. God interrupted Peter, showing that we must sometimes stop talking to hear Jesus clearly. God redirected Peter's focus, guiding him toward obedience.

In the Bible, noteworthy events on mountains are typically followed by movement. Consider the following examples:

- Moses descends from Sinai with the law.

- Elijah goes on to call Elisha from Carmel.

- Ezekiel delivers hard truths to the exiles.

Mountains are where we gain clarity, while valleys are where we apply it. The important thing is not merely to see incredible sights but to hear God's Word.

God interrupted Peter's plan to settle in. Why? Because mountaintop moments are not the end; they serve as training grounds, preparing us for the valleys that lie ahead. The very next scene after the mountain was chaotic: a demon-possessed boy the disciples could not heal and a desperate father pleading for help. This illustrates the reality of ministry.

The pattern is clear: after revelation comes responsibility. After moments of glory, we face the grind of life.

Peter's mistake was not excitement—it was misdirection. He confused the moment with the mission. God redirects him with three words: "Listen to Him." Obedience turns a spark into a flame and transforms moments into movements.

"The pattern is clear: after revelation comes responsibility. After moments of glory, we face the grind of life."

This is where we must step in as leaders, parents, and pastors. Our role is not merely to create environments where students meet God—it is to disciple them, so those encounters become obedient lives. If faith ends at the mountain, it stays personal. But if faith moves into the valley, it becomes powerful.

EXPECT VALLEYS AFTER MOUNTAINS

After every mountaintop, there is a valley. Spiritual highs do not exempt us from spiritual battles. Tim Keller writes, "Jesus comes down the mountain not to be admired but to enter suffering." One of the biggest mistakes we can make is treating the spiritual high as normal and the valley as abnormal. However, it is in the valleys that faith truly matures.

After the glory comes the grind, Jesus did not avoid it—He walked straight into it.

Students must understand that Monday morning matters as much as Sunday night. The real test of your faith is not how high you raise your hands in worship but how you treat people when no one is watching. The proof of the mountain is found in the valley.

So do not despise the valley; it is where movements are born.

"So do not despise the valley; it is where movements are born."

Remember What You Saw (2 Peter 1:16–18)

Years later, Peter reflected on that moment on the mountaintop. In 2 Peter 1, he writes: "We were eyewitnesses of His majesty… We ourselves heard this voice that came from heaven when we were with Him on the sacred mountain."

However, the key is this: Peter did not write about building tents; he wrote about proclaiming Jesus. That moment became his mission. We are called to do the same—not to freeze our faith in an emotional snapshot, but to carry it forward as a movement that changes lives.

FOR LEADERS, PARENTS, AND TEACHERS

Youth Leaders: Do not let camp be the peak. Build systems of discipleship that guide students from mountain moments into everyday missions.

Parents: Celebrate the encounter but then help anchor it. Ask your kids how they can apply it at school, with friends, and in their daily habits.

Teachers & Mentors: Remind students that what they have seen of God is not just for themselves; it is for the world they are sent into.

Do Not Let It End on the Mountain

Moments are sparks. They matter; they are holy. But they were never meant to be held onto. Peter wanted to build a tent, while Jesus wanted to make His Church. So, here is the choice: We can either build tents that keep us comfortable or build lives that move with God into the valleys.

The mountain shows us His glory, and the valley shows us His power. When students carry both, a moment becomes a movement

REFLECTION QUESTIONS

Where am I tempted to quit too soon?

What long-term fruits have I seen from staying the course?

*Who has modeled long obedience for me—
and what can I learn from them?*

How do I react when progress feels slow?

Conclusion

You then, my child, be strengthened by the grace that is in Christ Jesus, and what you have heard from me in the presence of many witnesses entrust to faithful men who will be able to teach others also"

2   Timothy 2:1-2

What A Time to Be Alive

For if you keep silent at this time, relief and deliverance will rise for the Jews from another place, but you and your father's house will perish. And who knows whether you have not come to the kingdom for such a time as this?" Esther 4:14

Big Idea: God placed us in this moment on purpose—the future is not something to fear but something to lead.

TIKTOK TO TESTIMONY

I came across an article about a woman named Alnissa Williams and her complicated relationship with her mother, which went viral on TikTok. According to the article, "Alnissa's relationship with her mother has been complex," she tells PEOPLE. Her mother became pregnant with her at 17 and gave birth when she was 18. After her parents separated, Alnissa's mother entered an abusive relationship that affected both.

Growing up, Alnissa experienced emotional and physical separation, which left deep, unresolved wounds. Over the years, they drifted apart, and Alnissa tried to bury her pain and move on. She believed time would heal their relationship or that there would always be a chance to make amends, but the years went by without any change.

A turning point for Alnissa came when she took a second job as a security guard, working the night shift across from a cemetery. During those nights, she found herself alone with her thoughts. She reflected, "You get a lot of time to think… and you start thinking about memories." As she looked at the gravestones in the quiet darkness, she felt the heavy weight of time. Each gravestone represented a life that had ended, and she realized that if she didn't act soon, she might lose the chance to reconcile with her mother. Confronted with this realization, Alnissa faced a choice: to let time slip away or to take a risk and make the most of the time she had left.

So, she decided. Alnissa set out on a 37-hour drive from California to Virginia to reconcile with her mother — to address the hurt, choose forgiveness, and rebuild their bond. Together, they managed to repair what was broken. Alnissa understood that time is not guaranteed; there is no promise of tomorrow — only the present moment.[62]

Alnissa's story reminds us not to wait until loss forces us to realize how much time we've wasted. Don't let the burden of lost time be what finally makes you wake up. Please don't wait until time runs out to start making the most of it.

Here is a truth for you: God placed you in this moment, this generation, and this city for a reason.

The political climate may feel chaotic, social media might seem overwhelming, and technology can complicate life, but none of this is accidental. God did not make a mistake in placing you here, at this moment.

It is easy to look around us and feel overwhelmed. Cultural tension, confusion, and pressure seem louder than ever. But Scripture tells a different story.

You were not born into this moment by accident. God has always worked through uncertain times, and He has always entrusted His people with responsibility in them. What a time to be alive.

"You were not born into this moment by accident. God has always worked through uncertain times, and He has always entrusted His people with responsibility in them."

The question is: will you recognize the time you have been given, or will you let it pass you by?

The danger we face is not merely about wasting time; it lies in the assumption that we will always have more of it.

Oswald Chambers powerfully reminds us, "The most important thing in the world is not time, but what we do with it. Time is, but a tool; how we use it determines our life." [63] This quote highlights the importance of our choices regarding time management. Time is a limited resource: you cannot buy, borrow, or create it. Our only decisions are whether to use it wisely or waste it.

Let's take a moment to pause and reflect: where are you choosing to spend your valuable time? More importantly, where might you be wasting it? In our busy lives, we often feel constantly occupied, rushing from one task to the next without taking a break. But what if our hectic schedules don't truly represent being busy, but instead reveal a deeper problem with how we manage our time?

The wisdom of Psalm 90:12 (NIV) urges us to, "Teach us to number our days, that we may gain a heart of wisdom." Additionally, Ephesians 5:16 (NIV) encourages us to "Make the most of every opportunity, because the days are evil." If we genuinely want transformation in our lives, we need to reevaluate how and where we spend our time.

Let us conclude as we began, with the story of Esther, recalling that she faced enormous challenges as her people faced danger, and time was running out. At this pivotal moment in her life, she faced a vital choice: how would she make use of the limited time she had?

The biblical story of Esther's situation, along with that of her cousin Mordecai, reveals a significant plan. Esther was supposed to reveal her Jewish background to King Xerxes and ask him to cancel a harmful order that endangered her people. However, she faced a daunting challenge: approaching the king without being summoned could mean her death. She had been living comfortably in royal luxury for five years, but now she was faced with a life-or-death choice.

Esther's brave response in chapter 4 serves as a powerful example for all of us when facing the call to act in situations that seem beyond our control. Her first reaction? A decisive "No!" During tough times, it can be hard to go beyond our self-centered instincts and focus on the larger mission Jesus has called us to complete.

This story challenges us to consider: How can we find the faith and courage to do what is right when we're overwhelmed by uncertainties and doubts? It asks us to reflect on where God is in our midst.

Interestingly, the book of Esther is unique because it does not explicitly mention God. However, even without His name, His divine presence is clearly evident.

John Nelson Darby once said, "God's ways are behind the scenes; but He moves all the scenes which He is behind."[64] This quote reminds us that we often waste precious time waiting for a divine sign or answer when, in fact, we might already have the guidance we need.

In Luke 17:20 (NLT), Jesus responds to the Pharisees' question about when the Kingdom of God will arrive: "The Kingdom of God can't be detected by visible signs." This indicates that we should stop waiting for obvious signs and instead start acting on the guidance God has already given us.

Esther's story encourages us to reflect critically on our lives: Are there relationships we've let go of? Have we missed opportunities that could help us grow? Are we ignoring our callings, clinging to the false hope that we'll have more time later?

It is crucial to realize that God has placed us in this specific moment in history for a clear and meaningful purpose. The way we choose to spend our time can significantly influence our lives and those around us.

Just as Esther boldly took action when she needed to, we must rise to the occasion and passionately pursue God's will without hesitation. The question is, how did she succeed in doing this, and how can we imitate her actions?

SPEAK UP, NOT STAY SILENT

Mordecai reminded Esther of an important truth: even though she was queen, her safety was not assured. The royal decree was straightforward — it called for the extermination of all Jews, and Haman, filled with hatred, would make sure that every Jewish person was hunted down. Mordecai strongly believed that God would find a way to deliver His people, but he warned Esther that she might become a victim of the looming danger if she stayed silent. The situation was grave; silence and inaction could lead to devastating results for her and her community.

God's divine purposes will succeed, even if His followers fail to act. If Esther decided to ignore God's plan for her life, His people would still find deliverance, but she would miss out on the blessings obedience could bring. She would lose an opportunity similar to Peter's, who, when called, let go of his fishing nets to follow a higher purpose.

We also need to consider the consequences of refusing to accept God's will. If we choose to do nothing, God might find someone else to carry out His plans, leaving us to miss out on rewards and divine favor. Alternatively, He may use discipline to bring us into obedience, as He did with John, Mark, and Jonah. John Mark gave up his mission, but God raised Timothy as his replacement. Jonah tried to run from God's command, but God's persistent pursuit eventually led him to obey.

Reflecting on this, I recall my own experiences — sitting on the sidelines while others participated fully in a project or a championship game. I disliked being the person who reaped the rewards without contributing. The feeling of watching life unfold without taking part was never appealing to me.

Now is the time to speak up. Our culture openly accepts sin; therefore, we must also be brave and vocal about our faith in our Savior. The reasons we often stay silent include societal opinion, fear of judgment, lack of confidence, and anxiety about possible consequences.

However, it is essential to remember that what God thinks of us is much more important than anyone else's opinions. As James 4:17 (NLT) reminds us, "Remember, it is sin to know what you ought to do and then not do it."

Take, for example, the "bystander effect," a well-documented psychological phenomenon where people are less likely to step in during an emergency, assuming someone else will act. A tragic and powerful example of this happened in 1964 with the murder of Kitty Genovese in Queens,

New York. Kitty was attacked and stabbed multiple times during a half-hour ordeal while 38 witnesses heard her cries but didn't intervene or call for help, highlighting the dangers of inaction. [65]

This reflects a more profound spiritual truth: many of us remain silent when God calls us to speak up. Esther faced a crucial decision — she could stay a bystander or become a brave advocate for her people. Similarly, we face this vital choice in our own lives.

Live Out Your Faith Authentically

People should recognize your commitment to Christianity not just through your words, but through the authenticity of your actions — let your life be your testimony!

TRUST THE ANOINTING, NOT ACCIDENTS

Understanding "anointing" is essential. It refers to being set apart or consecrated for God's purpose. After salvation, we receive the Holy Spirit, who unites us with Christ and shares His anointing.

Mordecai emphasized that Esther's rise to queenship was not a random event but a divine appointment. If God elevated her to the throne, there was a deliberate purpose behind it — one that has now become crystal clear: she was placed to intercede for her people.

Mordecai's well-known words, "Who knows? Perhaps you became queen for such a time as this," resonate deeply. Could it be that you are in your current situation for a purpose? During a time of possible genocide and oppression, Esther faced this challenge. Today, we might think about our own struggles — whether during war, political division, or the overwhelming influence of social media.

The phrase "Who knows?" appears repeatedly in the Bible, highlighting life's uncertainties and mysteries that often surpass human understanding.

King David, faced with the sorrow of losing his child with Bathsheba, responded, "Who knows? The Lord may be gracious to me, and the child may live." Similarly, when Jonah warned Nineveh of impending destruction, the king declared a fast, pleading with God, "Who knows?" in hopes of mercy for his people.

Mordecai's words to Esther remind us that her position as queen was ordained by divine providence, not by luck. This is equally true for each of us — we are not here by accident and have been chosen for the challenges and opportunities ahead.

When feelings of inadequacy overwhelm you or make you question whether you are capable, remember you have been chosen for this purpose. The Spirit of God dwells within you. You might not see the whole plan that God has prepared, but trust that He knows everything ahead—and that is enough.

TAKE A RISK, DO NOT RETREAT

Although the earthly king had set a dangerous precedent by forbidding Esther to approach him uninvited, her determination to obey her heavenly King remained firm. She resolved, "If I perish, I perish." In this moment of truth, Esther showed extraordinary courage, risking her position and life to fulfill her divine purpose.

We also face moments that require us to step out in faith, risking comfort and safety for a higher purpose. Just as Esther did, each of us can take a stand and embrace the role God has called us to, no matter the risks.

Do not miss the Moment.

It's easy to sleep through your moment. We can get distracted by responsibilities, discouraged by resistance, or disqualified by fear. Esther could have done the same. She could have stayed silent. She could have remained comfortable. But she realized something powerful: her silence would not protect her from the fallout of doing nothing.

That same challenge lands at our feet.

As youth pastors, parents, and leaders, we face a critical cultural moment. Students are seeking identity, hope, and belonging in all the wrong places. The noise of the world is amplified. The questions are more urgent. The pressure is mounting.

But that is why we are here. Because the Church does not shrink in darkness, it shines.

The world is watching—and so are the students. Every generation needs leaders who understand their responsibilities. Esther didn't show up at the palace by accident, and neither did you.

You might not feel like the most prepared, charismatic, or important voice in the room—but God isn't looking for perfect resumes. He's looking for surrendered hearts.

What is needed at this moment is leaders who are present.

Parents who stay faithful. Teachers who speak life. Students who choose bold obedience.

It may not seem like much in the moment, but those small, faithful decisions echo into eternity.

Now Is Not the Time to Shrink Back

If there is one thing Esther teaches us, it is that courage must be louder than comfort. The enemy will try to tempt you into believing you're too late or that you've missed your chance. Someone more talented, connected, or polished will step in. But let me remind you: God placed you here for a reason.

You may be the only person speaking truth in a student's life. You may be the one safe place in your child's week. You may be the quiet example of someone watching more closely than you think.

This generation does not need more influencers. They need intercessors.

They need disciple-makers. They need leaders like you, imperfect but present.

The times may be uncertain, but the calling is clear. God is still forming hearts, building His church, and calling leaders to stand faithfully in their generation.

Not because the moment is easy, but because God is present. Not because the path is clear but because the mission still stands. And not because we are strong but because He is faithful.

Lead the way.

REFLECTION QUESTIONS

What stories or lessons from this book had the most impact on me?

What does faithfulness look like in the season ahead?

*What is one bold step I will take because I
believe God called me to lead now?*

Who can I mentor, disciple, or invest in during the next 30 days?

ACKNOWLEDGEMENTS

This book would not exist without the people who have poured into me, walked with me, and believed in this message long before it hit the page.

To my wife, Daniela Mion—thank you for your unwavering love, strength, and support through every late night and early morning. You have seen the tears, the wrestling, and the breakthroughs—and you have carried it with me. This book is as much yours as it is mine. Your cover design is incredible! On to the next project!

To my kids, Eden and Jude, being your Dada is the joy of my life. I pray that this book becomes part of the legacy I leave for you.

To my parents – You are the most outstanding examples of following Jesus I have had my whole life. Mom, thanks for forcing me to go to that Youth camp.

To Pastor Alex Sagot, thank you for pointing out the leader in me when I could not see it myself. Your mentorship has shaped how I view ministry and leadership; your voice is clear throughout these pages.

To the Calvary Church staff, every youth and young adult leader, and every student I have had the honor of discipling—thank you for trusting me, challenging me, and showing me what it means to lead with grace and truth.

To my close friends and creative partners, Alex Perez, Ryan Sawal, Pastor David Campbell, María J. Ramírez Largo, and the students who shared their testimonies. Thank you for your feedback, encouragement, and care.

And finally, to the One who called me, sustained me, and never stopped authoring my story—Jesus. May this book bring glory to You and reach the ones You have placed on my heart.

AUTHOR BIO

Phil Mion is a pastor, writer, and creative communicator who is passionate about reaching the next generation. He graduated with a Bachelor of Science from Harding University and earned a master's in biblical studies from Liberty University. With over 14 years of experience in youth and young adult ministry, he helps students discover their identity in Christ and live it out in their daily lives.

Currently, Phil serves as the Executive Pastor at Calvary Church in Miami, FL, where he leads Next Gen ministries, creative teams, and large-scale conferences, including the Calvary Conference, Encounter Conference, and Legacy Parent Gathering.

Additionally, Phil is the founder of the Legacy Parent Network, a ministry that equips parents with tools to disciple their children in a digital age. Together with his wife, he hosts the "On the Way" podcast, where they discuss parenting, faith, and everyday life.

Phil and his wife are raising their two children, Eden and Jude, with grace, laughter, and plenty of coffee.

You can connect with Phil at:

Instagram: @philmion

Email: Phil@calvaryconnect.com

Threads: @philmion

Substack: https://substack.com/@philmion

REFERENCES

Introduction

1. Ortlund, Ray, and Jani Ortlund. 2024. To the Tenth Generation. B&H Publishing Group.

2. Barna Group, and Impact 360 Institute. 2018. Gen Z: The Culture, Beliefs and Motivations Shaping the next Generation. Ventura, Ca: Barna Group.

3. J. R. R. Tolkien. (1954) 2015. The Fellowship of the Ring. Vol. 1. Harpercollins Publishers Limited.

4. Spurgeon, Charles . 1874. "Providence—as Seen in the Book of Esther."

5. Hodges, Chris. 2025. "GrowLeader Podcast." Podcast . Spotify.

6. "One Hope Youth Ministry Roundtable." 2022. West Palm Beach: OneHope.

7. One Hope Youth Ministry Roundtable." 2022. West Palm Beach: OneHope.

8. "One Hope Youth Ministry Roundtable." 2022. West Palm Beach: OneHope.

9. "One Hope Youth Ministry Roundtable." 2022. West Palm Beach: OneHope.

10. "One Hope Youth Ministry Roundtable." 2022. West Palm Beach: OneHope.

11. Barna Group, and Impact 360 Institute. 2018. Gen Z: The Culture, Beliefs and Motivations Shaping the next Generation. Ventura, Ca: Barna Group.

Part 1 - Character

12. Comer, John Mark. 2026. "Leading through Apprenticeship." Catalystleader.com. 2026. https://insider.catalystleader.com/read/leading-through-apprenticeship.

Chapter 1 – The Power of a Self-Aware Leader

13. Miller, Kori D. 2020. "Using Self-Awareness Theory and Skills in Psychology." PositivePsychology.com. January 7, 2020. https://positivepsychology.com/self-awareness-theory-skills/.

14. Isaacson, Walter, and Steve Jobs. 2015. Steve Jobs. London Abacus.

15. Burgess, Olivia. 2023. "Only 15% of People Are Truly Self-Aware. Here's How to Change That. - the Forem." The Forem. April 10, 2023. https://theforem.co/only-15-of-people-are-truly-self-aware-heres-how-to-change-that/.

16. Leak, Ryan. 2022. Leveling Up. Thomas Nelson.

17. John Mark Comer. 2024. Practicing the Way. Colorado Springs: WaterBrook.

Chapter 2 – The Addiction of Applause

18. "Judy Garland, 47, Found Dead." 1969. Archive.nytimes.com. June 23, 1969. https://archive.nytimes.com/www.nytimes.com/books/00/04/09/specials/garland-obit.html.

19. Spurgeon, Charles . n.d. "Commentary on Matthew 6:1-4." Sermon.

20. "His Name Is Not Forgotten." 2025. The Heaton File. September 11, 2025. https://heatonkent.com/2025/09/11/his-name-is-not-forgotten/.

21. Roy, Steven C. 2011. What God Thinks When We Fail. InterVarsity Press.

Chapter 3 – Submission Helps the Mission

22. GaryNorth.com. 2015. "Memory Hole: When MacArthur Refused to Shake Hands with a Surrendering Japanese Official." Garynorth.com. September 2, 2015. https://www.garynorth.com/public/14226.cfm.

Chapter 4 – Character that is Consistent

23. "Pete Rose Quote: 'Creating Success Is Tough. But Keeping It Is Tougher. You Have to Keep Producing, You Can't Ever Stop.'" 2026. Quotefancy.com. 2026. https://quotefancy.com/quote/1391565/Pete-Rose-Creating-success-is-tough-But-keeping-it-is-tougher-You-have-to-keep-producing.

24. Wooden, John, and Steve Jamison. 1997. Wooden: A Lifetime of Observations and Reflections on and off the Court. New York: Mcgraw-Hill.

25. DJL. 2016. "Vocation in the New Year | ...In the Meantime." Davidlose.net. 2016. https://www.davidlose.net/2016/12/vocation-in-the-new-year/.

Chapter 5 – Worship that Works

26. Keller, Timothy. 2012. Every Good Endeavor: Connecting Your Work to God's Work. New York: penguin books.

27. Pepler, Conrad. 1942. "Why Work? By Dorothy Sayers. (Methuen: 1s.)." Blackfriars: 23 (273): 489–89. https://doi.org/10.1017/s1754201400052358.

28. King Jr, Martin Luther. n.d. "'The Three Dimensions of a Complete Life'."

29. "Sharpen Your Axe." 2026. Sermonillustrator.org. 2026. https://www.sermonillustrator.org/illustrator/sermon3b/sharpen_your_axe.htm.

30. Mabry, Adam. 2018. The Art of Rest. The Good Book Company.

31. Comer, John Mark, and John Ortberg. 2019. The Ruthless Elimination of Hurry: How to Stay Emotionally Healthy and Spiritually Alive in the Chaos of the Modern World. The Crown Publishing Group.

32. "Renovaré | the Secret of the Easy Yoke - Dallas Willard." n.d. Renovaré. https://renovare.org/articles/the-secret-of-the-easy-yoke.

33. Maxwell, John C. 2022. The 21 Irrefutable Laws of Leadership: Follow Them and People Will Follow You. Nashville: HarperCollins Leadership.

Chapter 6 – The Rhythms of Rest

34. "Global Youth Culture - a OneHope Research Study." 2021. 2021. https://www.globalyouthculture.net/.

35. "Marathon Man Akhwari Demonstrates Superhuman Spirit." 1968. Olympics.com. International Olympic Committee. October 18, 1968. https://www.olympics.com/en/news/marathon-man-akhwari -demonstrates-superhuman-spirit.

Part 2 – Community

36. Bonhoeffer, Dietrich. 2015. Life Together. London: Scm Press.

Chapter 9 – Finding Identity in Community

37. Zetter, Kim. 2010. "LifeLock CEO's Identity Stolen 13 Times." Wired. May 18, 2010. https://www.wired.com/2010/05/lifelock -identity-theft/.

38. Kuehne, Dale S. 2009. Sex and the Iworld - Rethinking Relationship beyond an Age of Individualism. Baker Publishing Group.

Chapter 10 – More than a Mentor

39. Barna Group, and Impact 360 Institute. 2018. Gen Z: The Culture, Beliefs and Motivations Shaping the next Generation. Ventura, Ca: Barna Group.

Chapter 11 – The Friend We Need

40. Engler, Dawn. 2017. ""Friendship Is Born at That Moment When One Person Says to Another, 'What!'" Medium. June 26, 2017. https://medium.com/@dawnengler/friendship-is-born-at-that -moment-when-one-person-says-to-anotherwhat-697e71d212e1.

41. Ross, Tim. 2026. "David and Jonathan." Youtu.be. Pillar Church. 2026. https://youtu.be/FUOATDjehPA?si=bEKzcNqMEvA4cF1Q.

42. "Why We Love Baseball: The Embrace." n.d. MLB.com. https://www.mlb.com/news/why-we-love-baseball-jackie-robinson-pee -wee-reese-moment.

Chapter 12 – Choose Your Friends Carefully

43. Nelson, Craig. 2024. "Olympics: Jesse Owens and Luz Long and a Message of Hope." BBC Sport. BBC Sport. July 16, 2024. https://www.bbc.com/sport/athletics/articles/cd1xlr5ewrro.

44. Plano, Catherine. n.d. "You Are the Average of the Five People You Spend Time With." Www.ellevatenetwork.com. https://www.ellevatenetwork.com/articles/9895-you-are-the-average-of-the-five-people-you-spend-time-with.

45. Howerton, Josh . 2026. "The Domino Effect of Relationships." Youtu.be. Life Pointe Church. 2026. https://youtu.be/s4Ugr8B-vnio?si=9KPBwCnUR4drp5oh.

Part 3 – Culture

46. Buzzard, Justin. 2014. "Justin Buzzard." Justin Buzzard. March 17, 2014. https://www.justinbuzzard.net/articles/2014/03/17/the-fire-triangle-of-church.

Chapter 13 – Language of the House

47. Groeschel, Craig . n.d. "What You Allow, You Promote—Stop Low Standards." Www.youtube.com. Accessed January 20, 2026. https://www.youtube.com/shorts/fG4tF4PwSxc.

Chapter 14 – Guarding the Culture

48. Lucado, Max, and Thomas Nelson Publishers. 1996. When God Whispers Your Name. Thomas Nelson.

Chapter 15 – No More Excuses

49. Smith, Jacquelyn, and Natalie Walters. 2016. "Most Bizarre Late-To-Work Excuses." Business Insider. January 29, 2016. https://www.businessinsider.com/most-bizarre-late-to-work-excuses-2016-1.

Chapter 16 – When Disciples Doubt

50. Zamperini, Louis, and David Rensin. 2014. Don't Give Up, Don't Give In. Harper Collins.

51. "Henry Drummond - Dealing with Doubt." 2025. Ochristian.com. 2025. http://articles.ochristian.com/article15229.shtml.

52. Aw Tozer. 2005. Knowledge of the Holy. Authentic Media.

53. "Matthew 14 - Ryle's Expository Thoughts on the Gospels - Bible Commentaries - StudyLight.org." 2025. StudyLight.org. 2025. https://www.studylight.org/commentaries/eng/ryl/matthew-14.html.

Chapter 18 – Courage Under Fire

54. "Refr Sports." 2022. Refrsports.com. 2022. https://refrsports.com/blog/the-influence-of-home-crowds-on-referees-does-fan-pressure-impact-decision-making.

55. Wells, David F. 1999. Losing Our Virtue: Why the Church Must Recover Its Moral Vision. Grand Rapids, Mi: W.B. Eerdmans Pub.

56. "The Poisoned Crackers | Ministry127." 2026. Ministry127.com. 2026. https://ministry127.com/resources/illustration/the-poisoned-crackers.

Chapter 19 – Faith That Stays

57. Liebelt, Jim. 2022. "Culture Post: 42% of Couples Found Their Lost Spark, Fell Back in Love on Vacation - HomeWord." HomeWord - Providing Help and Hope in Every Chapter of Your Family Story. November 4, 2022. https://homeword.com/jims-blog/culture-post-42-of-couples-found-their-lost-spark-fell-back-in-love-on-vacation/.

58. Liebelt, Jim. 2022. "Culture Post: 42% of Couples Found Their Lost Spark, Fell Back in Love on Vacation - HomeWord." HomeWord - Providing Help and Hope in Every Chapter of Your Family Story. November 4, 2022. https://homeword.com/jims-blog/culture-post-42-of-couples-found-their-lost-spark-fell-back-in-love-on-vacation/.

59. Sr, Michael Porter, and Michael Porter Sr. 2024. "Reviving Your Faith." Thecrossingchurch.com. March 19, 2024. https://info.the-crossingchurch.com/blog/reviving-your-faith.

60. Charles Spurgeon. 1901. "Christ Transfigured Face."

61. Wright, N T. 2004. Matthew for Everyone, Part 1. Westminster John Knox Press.

Chapter 20 – What a Time to be Alive!

62. https://www.facebook.com/peoplemag. 2025. "After Years of Not Speaking to Her Estranged Mother, Woman Drives 37 Hours Cross-Country to Mend Relationship (Exclusive)." People.com. 2025. https://people.com/woman-drives-37-hours-cross-country-to-mend-relationship-mom-viral-tiktok-exclusive-11693267.

63. Chambers, Oswald. 1963. My Utmost for His Highest. Barbour Publishing.

64. "Circumstances, Events, and God, J.N. Darby (#43750) - Bible Truth Publishers." 2026. Bibletruthpublishers.com. 2026. https://bibletruthpublishers.com/circumstances-events-and-God/john-nelson-darby-jnd/pd43750.

65. "McGill University." 2025. Office for Science and Society. October 3, 2025. https://www.mcgill.ca/oss/article/critical-thinking-history/bystander-effect-started-lie.